Cambridge Elements

Elements in Child Development
edited by
Marc H. Bornstein
Eunice Kennedy Shriver National Institute of Child Health and Human Development, Bethesda Institute for Fiscal Studies, London
UNICEF, New York City

SOCIALIZATION AND SOCIOEMOTIONAL DEVELOPMENT IN CHINESE CHILDREN

Xinyin Chen
University of Pennsylvania

CAMBRIDGE
UNIVERSITY PRESS

CAMBRIDGE
UNIVERSITY PRESS

Shaftesbury Road, Cambridge CB2 8EA, United Kingdom

One Liberty Plaza, 20th Floor, New York, NY 10006, USA

477 Williamstown Road, Port Melbourne, VIC 3207, Australia

314–321, 3rd Floor, Plot 3, Splendor Forum, Jasola District Centre, New Delhi – 110025, India

103 Penang Road, #05–06/07, Visioncrest Commercial, Singapore 238467

Cambridge University Press is part of Cambridge University Press & Assessment, a department of the University of Cambridge.

We share the University's mission to contribute to society through the pursuit of education, learning and research at the highest international levels of excellence.

www.cambridge.org
Information on this title: www.cambridge.org/9781009069373

DOI: 10.1017/9781009072380

First published 2023

A catalogue record for this publication is available from the British Library.

ISBN 978-1-009-06937-3 Paperback
ISSN 2632-9948 (online)
ISSN 2632-993X (print)

Socialization and Socioemotional Development in Chinese Children

Elements in Child Development

DOI: 10.1017/9781009072380
First published online: February 2023

Xinyin Chen
University of Pennsylvania
Author for correspondence: Xinyin Chen, xinyin@upenn.edu

Abstract: Children's early temperamental characteristics have a pervasive impact on the development of socioemotional functioning. Through socialization and social interaction processes, cultural beliefs and values play a role in shaping the meanings of socioemotional characteristics and in determining their developmental patterns and outcomes. This Element focuses on socialization and socioemotional development in Chinese children. The Element first briefly describes Chinese cultural background for child development, followed by a discussion of socialization cognitions and practices. Then, it discusses socioemotional characteristics in the early years of life, including temperamental reactivity and self-control, mainly in terms of their cultural meanings and developmental significance. Next, the Element reviews research on Chinese children's and adolescents' social behaviors, including prosocial behavior, aggression, and shyness. Given the massive social changes that have been occurring in China, their implications for socialization and socioemotional development are discussed in these sections. The Element concludes with suggestions for future research directions.

Keywords: socialization, socioemotional development, Chinese children, social change, cultural values

ISBNs: 9781009069373 (PB), 9781009072380 (OC)
ISSNs: 2632-9948 (online), 2632-993X (print)

Contents

One cannot herd with birds and beasts. If I am not to be among other men, then what am I to be?

— Confucius, *Analects*, xviii.vi

1 Introduction

Considerable individual differences in temperamental characteristics emerge among children in the early years (Kagan, 1998; Rothbart, 2011). In unfamiliar or challenging situations, for example, some children are relaxed and spontaneous, whereas others tend to be anxious and distressed, displaying vigilant and wary behaviors. Children also vary in their abilities to regulate or control their emotional and behavioral reactions according to circumstances and social demands: whereas some children can initiate, maintain, or inhibit particular actions to achieve certain goals, others have difficulties controlling their behaviors and, at the same time, exhibit negative emotions, such as frustration and anger, in response to barriers and requirements. These kinds of early characteristics may have a pervasive and enduring impact on the later development of social and cognitive functions (e.g., Rothbart, 2011). Indeed, temperamental reactivity, self-control, and other characteristics in infancy and toddlerhood are associated with adaptive as well as maladaptive developmental outcomes, including educational attainment, delinquency, and psychopathological symptoms, in the later years (Chen & Schmidt, 2015).

Despite their dispositional nature, socioemotional characteristics and behaviors develop in social and cultural contexts (Bornstein & Esposito, 2020; Bornstein & Lansford, 2019; Chen & French, 2008; Whiting & Edwards, 1988). Social and cultural factors may be involved in development through facilitating or suppressing specific behaviors. Social norms and cultural values may also affect the meanings of behaviors and shape their developmental patterns and outcomes (Bornstein, 1995). The role of social and cultural contexts may be reflected in the influence of general socialization conditions, such as childrearing goals and practices, as well as adults' and peers' attitudes and responses toward children's behaviors in social interaction on developmental processes.

This Element focuses on socialization and socioemotional development in the Chinese context. The Element first briefly describes Chinese cultural background for child development, followed by a discussion of socialization cognitions and practices. Then, the Element discusses socioemotional characteristics in the early years, focusing on temperamental reactivity and self-control, mainly in terms of their cultural meanings and developmental significance. Next, the Element reviews research on children's and adolescents' social behaviors, including prosocial behavior, aggression, and shyness. Given the massive social changes that have been occurring since the early 1990s in China, their implications for socialization and socioemotional development are discussed in these sections. The Element concludes with suggestions for future research directions. A number of studies have been conducted on socialization and socioemotional development with Chinese children in Western countries. Thus, the Element reviews and discusses the relevant literature and research on Chinese children in China as well as other countries.

2 Cultural Background for Child Development in Chinese Society

As a country with one of the most sophisticated and ancient civilizations in the world, China experienced various waves of population migration, amalgamation, and development over thousands of years, which generated distinctive cultural systems. Among the fifty-six ethnic groups in the country, Han Chinese represent about 91 percent of the population (The World Factbook, 2022). Although the cultures of minority nationalities, such as Zhuang, Hui, Uygur, and Tibetan, exert significant influence on social activities and individual behaviors, particularly in the Western regions of the country, Chinese society of Han nationality is relatively homogenous in its cultural background, with Confucianism serving as a predominant ideological guideline that emphasizes the importance of the family and social relationships. The research that is reviewed in this Element has been conducted mostly with Han children and families.

Traditional Confucian culture was rooted in agricultural life (e.g., rice farming, especially in South China), which relies highly on interpersonal cooperation and values rule-abiding and responsible behaviors (Greenfield, 2009; LeVine, 1988). Relative to other major ancient belief systems in China, such as Daoism and Buddhism, that concentrate on the spiritual aspects of human life, Confucianism is more interested in how people handle issues with others and, thus, is more relevant in directing individual behaviors in the family and other social settings. The primary concern of Confucianism is to maintain order and harmony in the society. To achieve this goal, people are encouraged to learn and engage in responsible behaviors that are conducive to the well-being of the group. A strategy to maintain social harmony is to establish a set of moral standards and rules for social activities and to require individuals to fulfill their roles in society by following those standards and rules (Luo, 1996). The doctrine of filial piety (孝), for example, stipulates that children must show absolute obedience to their parents and honor the elders in the family, whereas parents are responsible for teaching and disciplining their children. The effort of children to succeed is viewed as a filial duty for the family, and parents have an obligation to ensure that children receive adequate training to achieve success (Ho, 1986). Behaviors that threaten the harmony or the hierarchical structure of the family are strictly prohibited. In this context, the expression of individual desires and the pursuit of personal interests are discouraged, especially when they are in discord with group functioning. Confucian principles concerning social relationships and behaviors have been endorsed in Chinese and some other East Asian societies, such as Korea and Japan, and have exerted an extensive influence on child education and development.

Although the influence of Confucian and other traditional Chinese values has weakened since the beginning of the last century, the core of the cultural system, such as group orientation, is robust during social changes and continues to impact socialization goals and practices in the contemporary Chinese society (Chen, 2010). Group-oriented cultural values, as represented by Chinese collectivism, emphasize individuals as a part of a group, in which members are linked to each other but differ on within-group status, and encourage obedience to the authority and the sacrifice of personal interests for collective well-being (Oyserman et al., 2002). In the family, group orientation is represented by the common goal to enhance family reputation and emotional and financial interdependence of family members. Maintaining parental authority, particularly in childrearing, is believed to be essential to achieve the common goal and the success of the family (Chao, 1995; Ho, 1986). The organization of Chinese schools is also based on collectivistic principles. For example, students are required to participate in regular group activities that are organized by the school. These activities are believed to help students develop positive attitudes toward the group and learn cooperative skills and behaviors that promote group welfare. Indeed, group-oriented values (e.g., "It is important to do what the group decides," "I would give up something important for me if it is good for the group I am in") are highly endorsed by students in Chinese schools (e.g., $M = 4.01$ on a 5-point rating scale ranging from $1 = $ *not at all agree* to $5 = $ *always agree* in a urban sample; Liu, Fu, et al., 2018). Students who endorse more group-oriented values tend to obtain higher social status and achievement (Liu, Fu, et al., 2018), suggesting that these values function to help students behave according to prevailing social standards in China.

3 Family Socialization

In both traditional and contemporary Chinese societies, socialization agents, particularly parents, are expected to provide guidance, support, and training for children to develop group-oriented attitudes and behaviors. Researchers have attempted to identify the features of socialization beliefs and practices of Chinese parents and understand their role in childrearing and development. Compared with Western parents, Chinese parents pay greater attention to children's learning social standards and acquiring achievement in school settings (Chen, Fu, et al., 2019; Ng & Wang, 2019). Chinese parents tend to be highly involved in children's social and school activities, expecting children to comply with their directions and demands (Cheah et al., 2015). To ensure child compliance, parental involvement is often expressed in forms of high behavioral control, such as monitoring and restricting the child's activities, and psychological control, such as making the child feel bad when he/she disobeys (Chao & Aque, 2009; Chen et al., 1998; Fung & Lau, 2012; Jose et al., 2000).

Jose et al. (2000), for example, found in observations of family interactions that, compared with European American parents, Chinese parents displayed higher directiveness (e.g., parents made the decisions and children followed without question; parents quickly corrected children's errors). Similarly, Chao and Aque (2009) and Louie et al. (2013) reported that Chinese children rated their parents as stricter and more controlling (e.g., "Insist that I do exactly as I'm told") than Western children. Moreover, Jose et al. (2000) and Kho et al. (2019) found that Chinese parents are likely to yell and shout when children misbehave and to use punitive strategies such as restricting children's activities with little or no justification. Ng et al. (2007) also noted in observing parent–child interactions in learning settings that Chinese parents are less likely than US parents to praise children for success and concentrate on their mistakes. Chinese parents are more likely than US parents to point out when children fail on tasks and to stress the serious consequences. In addition, in communicating with children, relative to US parents, Chinese parents show less positive emotions and use more harsh parenting practices such as criticism.

Salient forms of psychological control among Chinese parents are shaming (e.g., tell children that they should be ashamed when they misbehave; tell children parents get embarrassed when they do not meet expectations) and guilt induction (e.g., tell children, "If you really care for me, you would not do things that cause me to worry"; Chao & Aque, 2009; Cheah et al., 2019; Fung, 2006; Louie et al., 2013; Wu et al., 2002). According to Fung (1999), shaming strategies include (1) verbal markers, such as social comparisons, (2) vocal cues, such as sighs and making disapproving sounds, and (3) nonverbal techniques, such as staring and frowning. Chinese parents often regard shaming and guilt induction favorably (Fung, 1999). Fung and Lau (2012) argued that Chinese parents use shaming and guilt induction to regulate children's misbehavior by highlighting the harmful effects such behaviors have on social relationships, which may promote children's attunement to the needs and feelings of others. Unlike European American parents, Chinese parents do not seem to be concerned that using these parenting strategies may have harmful effects on children's development of autonomy and self-worth. Chinese parents believe that shaming, guilt induction, and other power-assertive strategies can be used to teach children right from wrong and help them learn social responsibility and self-control (Chen, Fu et al., 2019; Fung, 1999; Ng et al., 2014).

3.1 Care-Based Power-Assertive Parenting

The power-assertive parenting style displayed by Chinese parents appears to fit into Baumrind's (1971) authoritarian category, which focuses on strict control, firm enforcement of rules, and child obedience. It is important to note that authoritarian parenting in Baumrind's theory is represented by parental high control as well as negative affect, such as low warmth, rejection, and hostility. Accordingly, the measures of authoritarian parenting typically include items that indicate, to a varying extent, negative parental emotional and behavioral reactions (e.g., "I explode in anger toward my child," "I use threats as punishment with little or no justification"; Lee et al., 2013) in addition to items assessing high control. Given the detrimental effects of parental rejection or unresponsiveness (e.g., Chen, Rubin, & Li, 1997; Rohner & Lansford, 2017), it is not surprising that authoritarian parenting assessed using these measures is associated with low competence and adjustment problems in Chinese children, which are similar to consequences for children from European American families (e.g., Chen, Dong, & Zhou, 1997; Dornbusch et al., 1987; Shen et al., 2018). The relatively high level of "authoritarian" parenting among Chinese parents and its associations with children's maladjustment seem to suggest that, as an outcome of this parenting style, Chinese children would generally display more social, behavioral, and academic problems than European American children, which is clearly inconsistent with the research findings (e.g., Chen & Tse, 2008; Dornbusch et al., 1987; Fuligni et al., 2005).

To address the discrepancy or so-called paradox, Chao (1994) argued that the parenting style that Chinese parents display should not be viewed as authoritarian because the power assertion that they use in childrearing is associated with care and concern, rather than unresponsiveness, coldness, or hostility. Chao (1994) used *guan* to characterize the mixture of directiveness, discipline, care, and concern in Chinese parenting. The word *guan*, which means "looking after" or "taking care of" in Chinese, was used earlier by Tobin et al. (1989, p. 93) to describe the attempt of Chinese teachers and parents to monitor and correct the impulsive and undercontrolled behaviors of "only" children who might be spoiled in the family due to the one-child-per-family policy that was implemented in China in the 1970s. The term typically refers to supervision and control over individuals, especially those who display problem behaviors, but Chao (1994) argued that it has positive connotations because they imply training, love, and governing. The conceptual ambiguity is illustrated in the measures of *guan*. The items in the measures (e.g., "Begin training child as soon as ready," "When child continues to disobey you, he/she deserves a spanking," "Allow child to sleep in parents' bed," "Emphasize neatness and organization," "Parents help child with studies"; Chao, 1994; Gao et al., 2015; Stewart et al., 2002) do not seem to reflect a coherent construct, as they tap a variety of beliefs and acts that are not necessarily connected with each other in a straightforward way. Moreover, studies of *guan* often arrived at inconsistent and confusing results (e.g., parents in Pakistan had higher scores than parents in the United States, who, in turn, had higher scores than parents in Hong Kong on *guan*; Stewart et al., 1998, 2002).

To capture and understand the distinct features of socialization in Chinese society and facilitate research in this area, based on Chao's and others' works (e.g., Chao, 1994; Cheah et al., 2019; Chen, Fu, et al., 2019; Stewart et al., 2002; Tobin et al., 1989), this section discusses a perspective of care-based power-assertive parenting (CBPAP) that deliberately and explicitly highlights two inherently connected aspects of parenting used by Chinese parents: care and power assertion. Care-based power-assertive parenting refers to parental expressions of care in power-assertive behavior or parental use of power assertion with care in childrearing. This parenting style may largely serve to help children develop socially valued behaviors and acquire achievement in group-oriented societies. It differs from authoritative parenting based on the combination of parental warmth and "child-centered" control, which is believed to mainly promote children's independence and autonomy in Western societies (Baumrind, 1971; Maccoby & Martin, 1983).

As a key element of CBPAP, parental care indicates attentiveness and concern of parents arising from a sense of heightened responsibility and associated anxiety to socialize children to succeed in the society. Unlike parental warmth in the Western literature, which is often manifested by outward and direct demonstrations and communications of positive emotions to enhance children's feelings of security, positive self-regard, and confidence to explore the environment (e.g., Bowlby, 1969; Maccoby & Martin, 1983), Chinese parents' care is typically expressed in terms of guidance and instrumental support (e.g., "I help and guide the child to develop good habits and be polite"; Cheah et al., 2015). The display of supportive behaviors is an indispensable component of parental care, which makes CBPAP different from "tough love" parenting – the use of stern, harsh, rigid, and perhaps unresponsive strategies with the intention claimed to help children in the long run. Chinese parents also tend to exhibit their care in forms of high involvement, sacrifice, investment, and worry about the child's failure to achieve social goals, which may lead to the use of power assertion.

The cultural values of individual freedom and autonomy in Western societies encourage parents to use power assertion with caution (Keller, 2020; Maccoby & Martin, 1983). In Chinese society, parental power assertion, including behavioral control and psychological control, is viewed as necessary; parents who do not exert adequate power assertion with children are regarded as irresponsible and incompetent (Chao, 1995; Chen, Fu, et al., 2019). However, the use of power assertion that is encouraged in Chinese families should be derived from parental care and directed to helping children learn social standards and appropriate behaviors, with the goal to maintain the harmony and well-being of the family and other groups. In other words, power assertion in CBPAP should not result from parental anger, hostility, coldness, or neglect. Thus, parental care-based power assertion is expected to facilitate children's development of competence, which is different from authoritarian parenting that weakens it (e.g., Baumrind, 1971). In short, parental care and associated concern may motivate Chinese parents to use power-assertive practices in interacting with children. At the same time, care-based parenting efforts are directed by group-oriented socialization goals and likely promote child development in socially relevant domains.

Cultural values of parental care-based power assertion also appear in children's perceptions of and reactions to parenting behaviors. Chinese children show less negative reactions to parental use of power assertion than their European American counterparts (Chao, 1995; Ho, 1986). Chao and Aque (2009), for example, found that Chinese adolescents reported lower levels of feeling angry with parental strictness and psychological control than European American adolescents did. Cheah et al. (2019) found that Chinese children and adolescents were likely to interpret parental use of high-power strategies in a positive manner (e.g., "For my own good"). Yu et al. (2019) also found that parental power assertion, in the forms of behavioral or psychological control (e.g., shaming, guilt induction), was associated with fewer problems or more positive outcomes in social and school performance in Chinese children, especially from families that highly endorse group-oriented values, than in European American children. Children's understanding and appreciation of parental care may allow them to benefit from the guiding function of CBPAP and, at the same time, reduce its potentially undesirable influence.

Parental emphasis on maintaining behaviors according to social standards, such as cooperation-compliance in social settings, may require constraining personal desires, which may not be readily appreciated by children, particularly at a young age. Moreover, relative to Western parents, Chinese parents tend to display lower levels of warmth and affection (e.g., smiling at the child, telling the child "I love you") in their interactions with children (Camras et al., 2008; Cheah & Li, 2010; Chen et al., 1998; Huntsinger & Jose, 2009; Wu & Chao, 2005).

When not appreciated by children, parental power assertion based more on care than on warmth may elicit dissatisfaction, anxiety, and other negative emotions, which may lead to relatively high levels of internalizing psychological problems in Chinese children (e.g., Zhong et al., 2013). Thus, relations between CBPAP and internalizing problems need to be examined in future research.

3.2 Strengthening in Adversity: A Chinese Belief about the Constructive Function of Adverse Experiences in Socialization

The inclination of Chinese parents to use power-assertive parenting, including shaming and guilt induction, may be related to a broad cultural belief in Chinese and some other East Asian societies about the constructive function of the experience of adversity in socialization (Leung & Shek, 2015; Li et al., 2021; Zhao et al., 2013). As an elaboration of human nature, Mencius (372–289 BC), one of the most famous Confucian thinkers, taught that "When Heaven is about to place a great responsibility on a man, it always first frustrates his spirit and will, exhausts his muscles and bones, exposes him to starvation and poverty, and harasses him by troubles and setbacks so as to stimulate his mind, toughen his nature, and enhance his competence" (Mengzi, Gaozi-Part II). A similar idea is expressed in an old Chinese adage "The fragrance of plum blossoms comes from the bitter cold," which is often used to inspire children to pursue long-term goals. From this view, the experience of adversity is beneficial for building socioemotional and cognitive strengths. Through the strengthening process, children with adverse experiences can develop better outcomes than children without such experiences. This view is similar to Friedrich Nietzsche's phrase "what does not kill me makes me stronger," although this phrase may not imply the experience of hardship as a necessary path to success. More importantly, the belief about the benefits of adverse experiences for child development is widely held and advocated in Chinese society and has had a widespread influence on childrearing in Chinese families, particularly those living in difficult conditions. Thus, a discussion of the socialization belief may help us better understand Chinese parenting.

The Chinese notion of strengthening in adverse circumstances differs from that of resilience in the psychopathological literature (e.g., Garmezy, 1971; Rutter, 1987), despite their overlap on improved performance of individuals who experience difficulties. Resilience generally refers to "the capacity of a dynamic system to withstand or recover from significant challenges that threaten its stability, viability or development" (Masten, 2011, p. 494). An important feature of the resilience theory is that it considers the experience of adversity a risk factor or disturbance to normal functioning. Children in adversity are expected to develop more problems than others. A separate attribute or process of resilience serves as a buffering factor that protects individuals who are exposed to risk from developing problems (Luthar et al., 2015). Researchers have recognized such phenomena as stress inoculation, steeling, and post-traumatic growth after adversity exposure (Bonanno, 2004; Rutter, 1987). In the context of risk, stress inoculation and steeling effects are largely concerned with the protective process that helps reduce or mitigate the negative impact of adversity.

The strengthening-in-adversity (SIA) belief suggests that the experience in adverse environments is useful and necessary for enhancing children's strengths and has constructive effects on development. The experience of adversity is regarded as an integral part of the strengthening process. It should be noted that adverse experiences that are considered constructive mainly refer to the experiences of living in difficult social, economic, and health conditions that are beyond parental or child control, such as the experience of social disadvantage and family economic hardship. The experiences typically do not include childhood maltreatment, such as psychological or sexual abuse and emotional or physical neglect (Luthar et al., 2021). Although a positive response to a particular negative or traumatic event (e.g., unexpected crisis, disaster, significant failure or loss) or a "turning-point" effect (Rutter, 2012) may be considered a type of strengthening, the SIA belief emphasizes the role of regular and cumulative experiences of challenges and difficulties in facilitating the development of competence and positive qualities in a progressive manner. Therefore, strengthening and associated changes in individual social and cognitive abilities should be understood from a socialization and developmental perspective.

Among the socialization practices that may facilitate the strengthening process (e.g., setting goals, planning, having a positive attitude toward difficult circumstances), helping children in adversity develop a sense of social responsibility and maintain strenuous effort has been stressed in the Chinese literature (e.g., Leung & Shek, 2016; Li et al., 2021; Luo, 1996). Adverse circumstances, such as poverty, are often shared by individuals in the environment, for example, family members, relatives, and residents in the community. As a long-term goal, children are encouraged to make contributions to improve the conditions (e.g., resources, opportunities, support systems) for the group, community, or society. Chinese parents also tend to value effort and hard work for achieving successful outcomes (e.g., Stevenson et al., 1990). Leung and Shek (2016) found, in a sample of families experiencing economic disadvantage in Hong Kong, that parental perceived importance of effort (e.g., "When my child does well in exams, it is most likely because he/she has put in effort," "Diligence is a means by which one makes up for one's dullness") is associated with positive attitudes about the role of adversity (e.g., "Hardship increases stature," "Man is not born to greatness, but he achieves it by strengthening himself"). Parental beliefs about effort and the role of adversity were both positively associated with expectations of children's future success (e.g., "I expect my child to complete university").

The belief about SIA has been discussed mostly for children from families with social and economic hardship (Leung & Shek, 2016; Li et al., 2021; Liu & Wang, 2018; Zhao et al., 2013; Zhao et al., 2016). For example, a significant issue in China in the early twenty-first century is massive internal rural-to-urban migration, which affects hundreds of millions of rural families. Children who migrate with their parents to the city and children who are left behind in the rural village by their parents are likely to experience social and psychological difficulties (Wang & Mesman, 2015; Wen & Lin, 2012). It is argued that these children should take the opportunity to hone their self-improvement skills based on their experience (Li et al., 2021; Liu & Wang, 2018; Zhao et al., 2016).

In a study conducted in public elementary schools in Shanghai, China, Chen, Li, et al. (2019) compared rural-to-urban migrant children with local urban nonmigrant children on social competence and academic achievement. Under the *hukou* system, migrant families do not have a legal registration status in the city and thus do not have the same rights and benefits (e.g., medical care, old-age pensions, employment opportunities) as local nonmigrant counterparts. Children from migrant families have fewer opportunities for future occupation and upward mobility. Moreover, migrant children are likely to experience stress and difficulties related to migration and adaptation to the urban environment, including negative perceptions and attitudes such as prejudice and discrimination from local people in the city. In the sample, over 60 percent of nonmigrant urban parents had an education of professional or technical school or undergraduate or graduate school, whereas approximately 90 percent of migrant parents had a senior high school or lower education. Urban nonmigrant families (approximately 13,000 Chinese yuan or US$2,000) had significantly higher monthly incomes than migrant families (approximately 7,600 Chinese yuan or US$1,100). Nevertheless, compared with urban nonmigrant students, despite their adverse social and financial circumstances, rural migrant students displayed greater social competence, as indexed by leadership status, peer acceptance, and peer- and teacher-assessed social skills. Moreover, rural migrant students attained higher academic achievement and had fewer learning problems. Among the migrant students, those who made a great effort to learn from new urban culture and engaged in active social interactions with urban peers were more likely to improve their social competence. The results, in general, seem to support the belief that the experience of adversity may have potential benefits for social and school achievement of rural migrant children, although the belief was not assessed in the study.

Limited research has been conducted about the SIA belief, mostly with rural left-behind children, rural-to-urban migrant children, and economically disadvantaged children (Leung & Shek, 2016; Li et al., 2021; Liu & Wang, 2018; Zhao et al., 2013). However, the belief about the value of adverse experiences in human development, which may or may not be true, is prevalent among Chinese parents and is an important part of the cultural system that provides a basis for the formation of socialization attitudes and practices in Chinese society (Leung & Shek, 2016; Luo, 1996). How the traditional cultural belief is integrated into childrearing is a question for parents in relatively wealthy urban families in China. Research has shown that with the rapid economic growth, children and adolescents have become more materialistic in many developed regions of China, such as Shanghai and Shenzhen, which is facilitated by the influence of consumerism (Fu et al., 2015). Moreover, children and adolescents who endorse materialism (e.g., "I really like the kids that have very special games or clothes," "It is important to have really nice things," "When you grow up, the more money you have, the happier you'll be") are more selfish and display less prosocial behavior toward family, friends, and strangers (Yang et al., 2018). Parents in urban families with better financial conditions are often concerned whether the lack of adverse experiences has a negative impact on the development of their children (Fu et al., 2015), which appears similar to the issue that is discussed in the literature about the risk of youth from affluent families (Luthar & Latendresse, 2005). Systematic research is needed on the socialization belief about the experience of adversity and its role in child development in Chinese and other societies.

3.3 Parenting Attitudes and Behaviors in the Contemporary Changing Chinese Society

Due to the massive economic reform, China has changed dramatically toward a competitive, market-oriented society, particularly in urban regions. Traditional socialization beliefs and practices are incompatible with the requirements of the market-oriented society that emphasizes individual initiative-taking, active exploration, and self-direction. To function adequately and obtain success in the new environment, individuals need to learn assertive, self-reliant, and autonomous skills (Chen & Chen, 2010). At the same time, Western individualistic values and ideologies, such as liberty and individuality, have been introduced into the country (Cai et al., 2020). The macro-level social and cultural transformations likely elicit and facilitate changes in parental attitudes and behaviors.

Zhou et al. (2018) conducted a semi-structured individual interview with grandmothers in Beijing about childrearing behaviors of three generations of parents in their families (their parents, themselves, and their children). Grandmothers (born in 1937–57) reported that their grandchildren (born in 1992–2014) received more parental support and praise for self-directed behavior than their children (born in 1958–92) and themselves did during childhood. Chen and Chen (2010) assessed childrearing attitudes of parents of elementary school children (ages nine to twelve years) in two cohorts (1998 and 2002) in Shanghai. Parents completed a measure tapping four dimensions of parenting: power assertion (e.g., "I do not allow my child to question my decisions," "I believe that scolding and criticism make my child improve"), encouragement of autonomy and independence (e.g., "I let my child make many decisions for him/herself," "I encourage my child to be independent of me"), parental warmth (e.g., "My child and I have warm, good times together," "I comfort my child when he/she is upset or afraid"), and encouragement of achievement (e.g., "I encourage my child always to do his/her best"). As shown in Figure 1, both mothers and fathers in the 2002 cohort had lower scores on power assertion than those in the 1998 cohort. Mothers in the 2002 cohort also had higher scores on autonomy support than mothers in the 1998 cohort. Parents in the 2002 cohort had higher scores on parental warmth than parents in the 1998 cohort. Finally, no differences were found between the cohorts on encouragement of academic achievement; parents at both times highly valued children's academic performance. Apparently, with the social change, parents in China encouraged more autonomous and exploratory behaviors and used less forceful and power-assertive parenting styles in childrearing. At the same time, they increasingly recognized the role of parent–child affective communication in promoting children's socioemotional competence and became more sensitive to child needs.

Chen, Chen, et al. (2021) examined maternal autonomy- and connectedness-oriented behaviors in a laboratory observational study of mother–toddler interactions in two cohorts (1995 and 2008) in urban China. Maternal encouragement of autonomy was indexed by mother's verbal and nonverbal behaviors that encouraged the child's initiation and continuation of exploration and self-directed play (e.g., "Wow, there are so many toys for you to play with. Why don't you go ahead and play?" "Would you like to play with the bunny by yourself?"). Maternal encouragement of connectedness was indexed by mother's verbal and nonverbal behaviors that encouraged the child's connectedness and affiliation, including engagement of common activities, expression of emotional closeness/communication with others, and physical proximity (e.g., "Do you want to build the house together with Mom?" "Bring the truck over, and play near Mommy"). Compared with mothers in the 1995 cohort, mothers in the 2008 cohort were less likely to display excessive involvement in children's activities and more likely to allow the

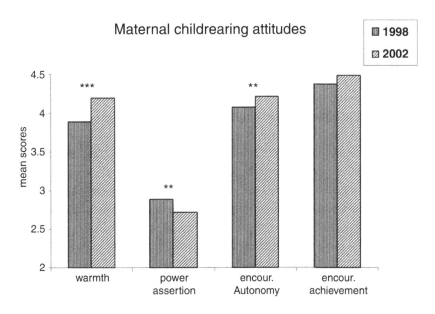

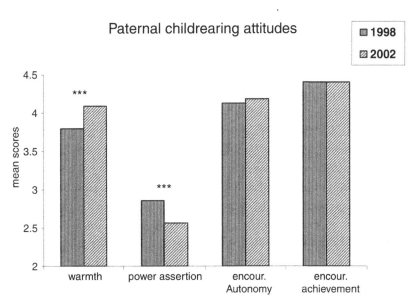

Figure 1 Parental childrearing attitudes in 1998 and 2002.
Note. ** = $p < 0.01$ and *** = $p < 0.01$ for differences between 1998 and 2002 cohorts.
Source: Based on data in Chen & Chen, 2010.

child to engage in activities without unnecessary interference. Moreover, after controlling for the overall involvement, mothers in the 2008 cohort displayed significantly more autonomy-supporting behaviors than did mothers in the 1995 cohort. Mothers in the 2008 cohort were more likely to encourage children to explore the environment and act independently than mothers in the 1995 cohort.

Compared to urban regions, rural regions in China have experienced fewer social changes because the massive economic reform, such as the opening of stock markets, has been largely limited to urban centers and cities. Families in rural China have lived mostly agricultural lives, and rural people, accounting for approximately half of the population in the country, do not have as much exposure as their urban counterparts to the influence of the dramatic social changes. In many rural areas, traditional values, such as those of self-constraint, cooperation, and obedience to the authority, are still emphasized in family socialization and education and continue to guide social activities (e.g., Chen et al., 2010). Rural adults and children are more likely to endorse group orientation and are less likely to pursue individual interests than their urban counterparts (Zhang & Fuligni, 2006). Parents in rural families tend to maintain socialization goals and use parenting practices that are consistent with the traditional beliefs and values, such as respect for elders and self-sacrifice for the family. Chen and Li (2012) investigated parental encouragement of initiative-taking in a sample of school-age children (*M* age = 11 years) from rural and urban families in a suburban region of a city in South China. The sample also included a group of children from urbanized families (i.e., families that changed from rural status to urban status due to the expansion of the city to the surrounding rural areas). Parents were asked to complete a measure about encouraging children to actively participate in social activities and display self-direction in the activities (e.g., "I encourage my child to take the lead in initiating activities," "I encourage my child to express his/her opinions in school and other public places," "I encourage my child to be independent and solve problems by himself/herself"). Urban parents were more likely than rural parents to appreciate and encourage initiative-taking in childrearing. Moreover, parents in urbanized families, which initially had the same background as rural families, became similar to their urban counterparts and had significantly higher scores on encouragement of initiative-taking than did rural parents. According to Chen and Li (2012), urbanized parents may have realized that as a result of the change in family status, their children need to develop new qualities and skills, including initiative-taking, that are important for achieving success in a more competitive urban environment.

Chen et al. (2010) examined parental perceived social change and adolescent-reported parenting attitudes and practices in rural and urban regions of China. Rural adolescents reported lower parental encouragement of independence and

higher parental control than urban adolescents did. Moreover, regression analyses revealed that parental perceived social changes in terms of opportunities
and prospects (e.g., "There are more job opportunities for me," "New technolo-
gies allow me to obtain more knowledge") positively predicted parental encouragement of independence and parental warmth in both rural and urban groups.
Thus, parents who perceive more challenges and opportunities to pursue personal career goals and to obtain new life experiences are more likely to encourage their children to develop independent behaviors and use affectionate and
sensitive parenting practices in childrearing. The beliefs that there were
increased job opportunities and, at the same time, high levels of competition
might motivate parents to help their children learn exploratory and initiative-
taking skills through intimate parent–child interactions and affective communications. In addition, in the rural group, but not in the urban group, fathers'
perceptions of new values (e.g., "My views and values are more influenced by
foreign cultures," "The knowledge and experience of my parents offer fewer
clues for my life today") were positively associated with control, and fathers'
perceptions of work-related risk (e.g., "When I review the last five years, I have
a higher risk of losing my job," "It is more difficult to plan my career for a long
term") negatively predicted encouragement of independence. Thus, rural
fathers who perceived the threat of new values, mostly from Western countries,
Hong Kong, and Taiwan, might think that they need to exert control on their
children. Rural fathers who perceived greater risk and adversity due to the social
changes were also less likely to encourage their children to develop independent
behaviors. Parents in rural regions might be particularly anxious about adverse
consequences of social changes and thus might be reluctant to encourage their
children to learn and display independent and exploratory behaviors.

4 Peer Socialization

In Western societies, peer interactions and relationships are considered an
important social context in which children develop autonomy and individuality
when they pursue psychological separation from parents (Larson, 1999; Rubin
et al., 2015). Peer relationships are a main source of emotional support and
stimulation that nurture the process of separation from the family. During peer
interactions, children are encouraged to display independence and acquire
personal identity while maintaining positive relationships with others (Hartup,
1989; Rubin et al., 2015). Striving for personal autonomy and individuality is
viewed as socially irrelevant or unacceptable in Chinese society (Chen, 2010).
The significance of peer relationships in Chinese children is appreciated mostly
in terms of its role in helping children learn skills and behaviors that can

contribute to group well-being (Chen, Lee, et al., 2018). Children are encouraged to maintain strong peer affiliations and learn from each other through participating in peer activities.

4.1 Friendships and Peer Groups

The literature in China on peer relationships, particularly friendships, is rich. Friendships are included in the Confucian five cardinal relationships ("wu lun"), along with relationships for ruler and subject, father and son, husband and wife, and elder brother and younger brother. Popular proverbs such as "Relying on your parents at home, and friends outside" point out a general belief about the importance of friendship. In the famous historical novel *Romance of the Three Kingdoms*, three friends in the Han Dynasty (AD 23–220) were described as so dedicated and loyal to each other that they wished to die on the same day. In swearing brotherhood in the Peach Tree Garden, they promised to help each other and work together for the common goal to "save the troubled, aid the endangered, and avenge the nation above and pacify the citizenry below."

Like their counterparts in Western and other countries (Chen, He, et al., 2004), the majority of children and adolescents in China, ranging from 70 percent to 90 percent, have friendships based on mutual nominations, with average numbers of mutual friendships ranging from 1.5 to 2.5 (Chen, Lee, et al., 2018; Huang et al., 2022; Li et al., 2017). More girls than boys form mutual friendships, and girls' friendships tend to be more stable over time (e.g., Chen, Lee, et al., 2018, Chen, et al., 2022). Children who have mutual friendships are more socially and academically competent and psychologically better adjusted than children without mutual friendships (Chen, He, et al., 2004, Chen et al.,2022). Chen et al. (2022) found in a large sample in China that approximately 40 percent of students in elementary schools (*M* age = 11 years) maintained stable mutual friendships over one year, which is substantially higher than the rates in the United States and many Western countries (e.g., Spithoven et al., 2018). The higher stability of friendships in Chinese children is due to the fact that students typically stay in the same class composition when they move to higher grades in elementary or high schools, whereas the composition changes during the transition from one grade level to the next in Western schools. In the Chinese interdependent or collectivistic cultural context, friendship is often regarded as inseparable from the self, allowing individuals within the relationship to readily regulate each other's behaviors and exert influence on each other's development (Chen, Lee, et al., 2018). Relatively stable friendships that Chinese children form exert significant influence on individual behavior and development (Chen, Lee, et al., 2018).

Researchers who study children's and adolescents' friendships have been interested in friendship qualities or provisions, such as intimacy, enhancement of self-worth, and instrumental assistance (e.g., Rubin et al., 2015). There are different views about culture and friendship intimacy. Triandis et al. (1988), for example, argued that friendships are more intimate in cultures which more highly value interpersonal connectedness and mutual support. By contrast, Sharabany (2006) argued that friendships may be lower in intimacy in more collectivistic cultures because of the availability of other sources of emotional support and the potential threat of friendships to the cohesiveness of the family and larger groups. Findings from several studies appear to suggest that children and adolescents in China have more intimate friendships than their counterparts in some other countries. For example, Liu, Li, et al. (2015) found that high school students in China reported a higher level of intimacy (e.g., "How much do you talk to this person about things that you don't want others to know?," "How much do you share your secrets and private feelings with this person?") than students in Indonesia did, although adolescents in Indonesia tend to have friendships that are relatively low in intimacy (e.g., French et al., 2005). Way (2006) also noted through interviews that, relative to European American adolescents, Chinese American adolescents were more likely to share their intimate feelings with friends.

A major function or provision of friendship in Western cultures is enhancement of self-worth or self-validation (e.g., "My friends make me feel important and special"; Furman & Buhrmester, 1985). However, children in China rarely mention self-validation as a main reason for friendship (e.g., Chen, Kaspar, et al., 2004). In contrast, instrumental assistance, particularly helping solve academic problems and learning social skills, is regarded by Chinese children as important for friendship. For example, a clear theme that emerged from the interviews with Chinese children is the great appreciation of mutual assistance of friends in performance on academic and social tasks in school (Chen, Kaspar, et al., 2004; Way, 2006). Compared with Western children, Chinese children are also more likely to communicate with friends about their academic achievement (Heyman et al., 2008). Disclosure and communication about academic achievement are believed to motivate children to study harder and indicate request or offer of assistance on academic tasks. A striking finding of Heyman et al.'s (2008) study was that, when presented with a scenario in which a student disclosed a positive performance to a poorly performing friend, the majority of children in the United States (86 percent) interpreted the disclosure as showing-off ("I'm better than you"), but the majority of children in China (68 percent) interpreted it as trying to help ("I can help you to do better"). According to Heyman et al. (2008), the responses of the children in the two countries might be related to the understandings and experiences of different cultural norms concerning self-presentation or self-enhancement and obligation to help friends to improve their academic performance.

Beginning in middle childhood (ten or eleven years of age), most of peer interactions in children take place in groups (Chen, Lee, et al., 2018; Rubin et al., 2015). Peer groups, formed spontaneously out of common interests, are networks of interacting individuals who spend time together and share activities. Frequent contact, joint activities, and affective connectedness among group members make peer groups a strong socialization influence in schools and neighborhoods (Kinderman & Gest, 2018). The nature of peer groups is particularly emphasized in Chinese culture in terms of whether group activities are guided by the "right" social goals. "Good" groups are believed to be represented by the endorsement of members on activities according to social standards. Groups that are considered high-quality in providing emotional closeness in the literature (e.g., Rubin et al., 2015) may have harmful influence on individual development if group activities are directed by antisocial goals (Chen, Lee, et al., 2018).

Chen and colleagues' studies (Chen et al., 2008; Liu et al., 2023) showed that approximately 90 percent of school-age children in China belong to peer groups, with average group sizes ranging from five to seven members. Peer groups in Chinese schools tend to be formed on academic norms and have contagion effects on children's behaviors within the academic domain (e.g., high-achieving groups promote members' academic achievement) as well as cascading effects on children's adjustment in other domains (e.g., high-achieving groups promote members' prosocial behavior and social status). Liu et al. (2023) examined socially competent peer groups and their contributions to individual development in a one-year longitudinal study with Chinese elementary school children. As social competence (e.g., sociability, social initiative-taking) is increasingly valued in the Chinese society, children are encouraged to engage in socially competent activities in peer groups, and socially competent groups are likely to obtain increased resources in school and instrumental and emotional support from adults and peers. The multilevel analysis revealed that group-level social competence had significant same-domain effects on later individual social competence. Group-level social competence also had a positive cross-domain effect on later individual academic performance and a negative cross-domain effect on later individual psychological problems (Figure 2). Moreover, the impact of social competence on development is manifested mainly at the group level, as indicated by the stronger and more extensive same-domain and cross-domain effects of group social competence than those of individual-level social competence on

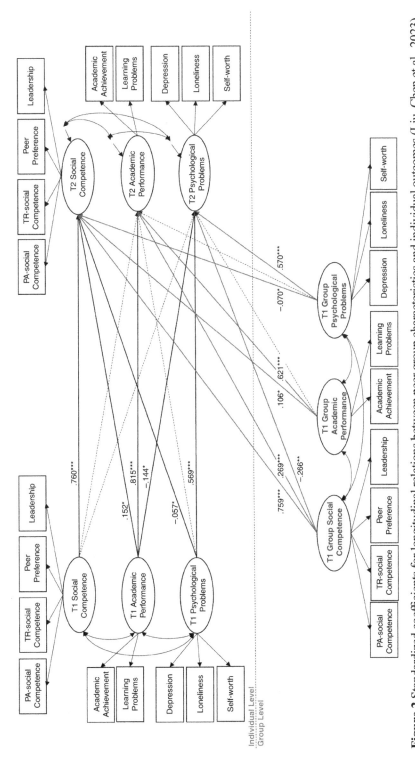

Figure 2 Standardized coefficients for longitudinal relations between peer group characteristics and individual outcomes (Liu, Chen et al., 2023). **Note.** Significant paths are represented by solid lines. PA = peer-assessed. TR = teacher-rated. Group gender and group size were controlled at Level 2.
* $p < 0.05$. ** $p < 0.01$. *** $p < 0.001$.

academic performance and psychological problems. As Liu et al. (2023) noted, interactions and activities in socially competent groups serve as a social milieu for the fulfillment of group influence on individual development.

4.2 Social Evaluation and Regulation in Peer Interaction and Individual Social Sensitivity

Developmental theories (e.g., LeVine, 1988; Vygotsky, 1978) have traditionally emphasized the socialization role of adults, especially parents and educators, in transmitting cultural values to the young generation. Chen (2012) argued that the process of cultural influence on development, particularly in socioemotional areas, is more complicated than internalization of cultural systems or learning from senior members of the society. According to the contextual-developmental perspective (Chen, 2012, 2020), social interactions in the peer context are an indispensable mediator of the links between cultural values and children's socio-emotional functioning, especially as children engage in more activities outside the home and classroom with age. From this perspective, cultural values are inter-twined with evaluation and response processes in peer interactions, which, in turn, regulate children's behaviors and their development. Specifically, when children display behaviors in social interactions, peers may interpret and evaluate those behaviors according to cultural norms and values. Peers may also respond to the behaviors by expressing their attitudes (e.g., approval or disapproval) toward the children, which are reflected in their relationships (e.g., acceptance, rejection, group affiliation, and leadership status). Positive evaluations inform children that their behaviors are regarded as appropriate and should be main-tained, and negative evaluations place pressure on the children to control or change their behaviors.

The intrinsic needs for social connection, intimate relationships, and group belonging are the main motivational forces that drive children to engage in interactions with others and to attend to and reflect on others' views and evaluations about them. Due to development in socioaffective brain circuitry and mentalizing (Somerville, 2013), children become particularly vigilant to real or perceived social evaluations in late childhood and early adolescence. As their social-cognitive abilities become increasingly sophisticated with age, children are also more capable of detecting, interpreting, and processing others' evaluations (Somerville, 2013). There are also individual differences in social sensitivity – the tendency to be attentive or vigilant to social evaluations. Whereas some children are highly attuned and responsive to social evaluations by peers, others are unable or unwilling to pay attention to social feedback on their behaviors (Chen et al., 2016).

Social sensitivity may not be in keeping with the socialization goal of pursuing independence and self-identity in Western cultures, despite the potentially constructive regulatory function of peer evaluations in individual development. In the Western context, children may feel the tension between their own needs and peer constraints (Rubin et al., 2015), and high social sensitivity may heighten these feelings, leading to social anxiety and distress (Westenberg et al., 2004). Moreover, socially sensitive children are often perceived as incompetent and immature because sensitivity to others' views and associated concerns about gaining approval from others are regarded as indicating low self-confidence and autonomy (e.g., Rudolph & Conley, 2005). In Chinese and some other East Asian group-oriented societies, such as Korean and Japanese societies, how one is viewed by others is considered more important than how one views himself/herself (Henrich et al., 2001; Kim et al., 2010). Individual sensitivity to others' evaluations is believed to be critical for children to solve problems with others, stay in accord with social environments, and eventually benefit from peer socialization (Heine et al., 2008; Henrich et al., 2001). Socially sensitive children are regarded as modest, considerate, and competent and are respected by others in China.

Chen et al. (2016) and Chen, Fu, et al. (2018) examined social sensitivity and its relations with indexes of adjustment among elementary and middle school children of different backgrounds in Canada and China. Social sensitivity was assessed using self-report and peer-assessment measures (e.g., "Think a lot about what other kids say about me (him/her)," "Always want to know what other kids think of me (him/her)," "Feel that it is important to know what other kids say about me (him/her)"). Different patterns of the relations were found in the two samples. Social sensitivity was positively associated with adjustment problems, such as peer rejection, teacher-rated incompetence, low self-esteem, and feelings of loneliness, in Canadian children. However, social sensitivity was positively associated with social and school adjustment, such as quality of peer relationships, teacher-rated competence, and academic achievement, in Chinese children. The positive relations were more evident in rural children than in urban children in China. Moreover, self-reported social sensitivity was negatively associated with loneliness and depression in rural Chinese children, but positively associated with loneliness and depression in urban Chinese children (although the magnitudes of the associations were smaller than those in Canadian children). Whereas their counterparts in Canada are vulnerable to socioemotional difficulties, socially sensitive Chinese children, particularly in rural China, achieve better developmental outcomes than others. In a society where sensitivity to social evaluations is encouraged, it is important for children to attend to and appreciate others' views about their behaviors. Supportive social and cultural environments provide opportunities for socially sensitive children to improve their performance based on social feedback. The mixed experiences of socially sensitive urban Chinese children appear to indicate the implications of the transition from the traditional group-oriented value system to the new Western self-oriented value system in urban regions of China. Urbanization and associated cultural changes may be weakening the adaptive value of social sensitivity in contemporary urban Chinese children's development.

In short, family and peer socialization practices in Chinese society, such as CBPAP and peer evaluation processes, exhibit culturally relevant features. To achieve socialization goals, adults and peers may exert influence on individual development through expressing culturally directed attitudes and reactions toward specific characteristics and behaviors that children display in social interactions.

5 Early Socioemotional Characteristics and Their Developmental Significance

Chinese children may display distinct socioemotional characteristics in the early years of life. Compared with their Western counterparts, for example, Chinese infants and toddlers tend to be less emotionally expressive and less active in social interactions (Camras et al., 1998; Chen et al., 2006; Wang, 2008). According to Chen and French (2008), the differences between Chinese and Western children on socioemotional characteristics in the early years may be characterized systematically by the dimensions of temperamental reactivity and self-control in social situations.

5.1 Temperamental Reactivity

Reactivity is concerned with how children respond to external stimuli, particularly challenging situations, in terms of the extent to which physiological arousal, approach versus avoidance behavior, and positive versus negative affect are elicited by the situations (Rothbart, 2011). A specific type of reactivity that has received much attention in developmental science is behavioral inhibition, which focuses on fearful reactions of infants and toddlers to novelty (Kagan, 1998). Chinese children have a higher level of reactivity to novel situations than North American children do. Ahadi et al. (1993), for example, found that, based on parental ratings, Chinese children were less active and more fearful in unfamiliar settings than US children. Based on laboratory observations of mother–child free play and interaction with a stranger, Chen et al. (1998) found that Chinese toddlers were more inhibited and vigilant in stressful settings than Canadian toddlers. Specifically, Chinese toddlers were less likely to explore the environment and stayed closer to their mothers. Moreover, Chinese toddlers displayed more anxious and fearful behaviors in interaction with the stranger, as indicated by their greater latency to approach the stranger and touch toys when they were invited to do so.

Initial research evidence suggests that reactivity in Chinese children is related to electrocortical, autonomic, and neuroendocrine processes that are similar to those in Western children (e.g., Ip et al., 2021; Xu et al., 2009a). Xu et al. (2009a) found in Chinese children that reactivity to stressful situations was negatively associated with heart period, which refers to the interval between heartbeats or the time for one cardiac cycle. Consistent with the Western literature (e.g., Fox et al., 2005), highly reactive Chinese children are sensitive and vigilant to novel stimuli, as indexed by exhibiting shorter heart period or faster heart rate. Doan et al. (2017) found that Chinese children had higher levels of cortisol in stressful settings than US children, which was consistent with findings based on parental reports and observations (Ahadi et al., 1993; Chen et al., 1998).

Findings concerning the genetic basis of temperamental reactivity in Chinese children are more complex. For example, research based on Western samples suggests that, despite the mixed findings of some studies, individuals with the short allele of the serotonin transporter genetic polymorphisms (5-HTTLPR) tend to display a higher level of fearful and anxious reactivity (e.g., Fox et al., 2005). However, Chen et al. (2014) found that Chinese toddlers with the short allele of the 5-HTTLPR were less fearful and anxious in reaction to the novel situation than their counterparts with the long allele of the 5-HTTLPR. Chiao and Blizinsky (2010) argued that cultural values, such as group harmony and conformity, in collectivistic societies may serve an "anti-pathogen" function by creating an environment that protects the majority of individuals, particularly those who are vulnerable, from developing maladaptive outcomes. Supporting this argument, analysis of data from twenty-nine nations showed that, whereas a high proportion of people in East Asia (70–80 percent of the population, compared with 40–50 percent in European samples) carried the short allele of 5HTTLPR, collectivistic values buffered against the exhibition of anxiety among East Asian people of short allele carriers (Chiao & Blizinsky, 2010). Nevertheless, it remains unclear how the gene-by-culture interaction explains the display of relatively low reactivity by children with the short allele of 5HTTLPR. Chen et al. (2014) argued that the associations between 5-HTTLPR alleles and reactivity in Chinese and Western children might be related to different cultural meanings of reactivity.

Chen et al. (1998) examined relations between toddlers' behavioral inhibition and maternal childrearing attitudes in China and Canada. Their analysis indicated that child inhibition was positively associated with mothers' negative attitudes, such as concern, disapproval, and rejection, in Canada, but with mothers' accepting attitudes, such as warmth and encouragement, in China. Parents in Canada are disappointed and frustrated with inhibited behavior that their children display and may express their negative emotions in parent–child interactions, which is consistent with the findings of other studies in Western countries (e.g., Rubin et al., 2009). However, parents in China view inhibited behavior as normal and appropriate, rather than incompetent or problematic. As a result, inhibited Chinese children tend to be accepted and supported by their parents and live in a favorable home environment.

Chen et al. (2006) observed peer interactions of four-year-old children in the laboratory situation in China and Canada and found that inhibited behavior was associated with different peer attitudes in the two countries (Figure 3). In Canada, peers were likely to display overt refusal, disagreement, and intentional ignoring (e.g., walking away; "You can't play because it's not your turn!") in response to social initiations made by inhibited children than by noninhibited children. In China, however, peers made more positive responses, such as cooperation, agreement, and compliance (e.g., offering help; "I really like drawing"; "Okay, I'll play"), to social initiations from inhibited children than from noninhibited children. Peers also made different voluntary initiations to inhibited children in the two countries: whereas peers in Canada made more coercive initiations, such as prohibition and direct demands (e.g., grabbing toys; "Gimme that") to inhibited children than to noninhibited children, peers in China made similar initiations to inhibited and noninhibited children. Thus, unlike their counterparts in North America, children who display high temperamental reactivity in China likely have positive experiences in peer interactions, which constitutes a social environment for adaptive development.

Longitudinal research in China has shown that temperamental reactivity in the early years is associated with social competence, school achievement, and psychological adjustment later in childhood and adolescence (Chen, et al., 2009; Chen, Fu, 2021). For example, behavioral inhibition in toddlerhood significantly predicts cooperative behavior in peer interactions, peer liking, perceived social integration, and positive school attitudes in middle childhood (Chen et al., 2009). Inhibited toddlers display more cooperative behaviors and have better peer relationships and psychological functioning in the later years than others. Inhibited toddlers are also rated by teachers as more competent in school performance and have fewer learning problems in elementary school. Moreover, early behavioral inhibition predicts social competence and academic achievement in late adolescence (Chen, Fu, et al., 2021). Peer relationships in middle childhood serve to buffer against the development of psychological problems of inhibited children. Inhibited children may be vulnerable to

Responses received from others

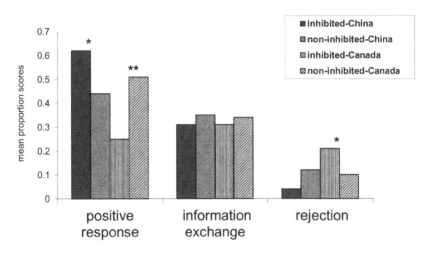

Initiations received from others

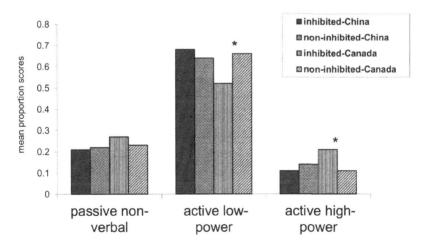

Figure 3 Responses and initiations inhibited and noninhibited children received from others in peer interactions in China and Canada.

Note. * = $p < 0.05$. ** = $p < 0.01$ for differences between inhibited and noninhibited children within the Chinese or Canadian sample.

Source: Based on data in Chen et al. (2006).

psychological distress and have a tendency to develop internalizing problems (e.g., Kagan et al., 2007). However, social support that inhibited children obtain and positive relationships they establish with others in childhood and adolescence in China protect them from developing problems.

5.2 Self-Control

Self-control is concerned with the ability to manage (e.g., initiate, maintain, modify, delay, or constrain) particular behaviors to achieve certain goals or respond to situational demands (Kopp, 1982). Research has shown the comprehensive impact of self-control on socioemotional and cognitive development (Mischel et al., 1996; Rothbart, 2011). Whereas a high level of self-control positively predicts later academic performance, cooperative behaviors, and quality of social relationships, a lack of self-control positively predicts maladaptive outcomes, such as learning difficulties and behavioral problems (e.g., Eisenberg et al., 2006). Therefore, helping children learn self-control is a major socialization task in most societies, often starting when children demonstrate an awareness of social demands and the capability to direct their behavior (Chen & French, 2008; Maccoby & Martin, 1983).

Self-control is a highly valued attribute in Chinese society because of its crucial role in the development of social behaviors, such as compliance with group norms, fulfillment of social responsibility, and suppression of individual desires. According to the traditional Confucian principles, children should be trained to follow the dictates of *li* (propriety) – a set of rules for actions – to cultivate and strengthen their innate virtues. During this process, children need to learn how to control their impulsive behaviors so they can better attend to the interests of others and the group. Self-control in children is typically indicated by their behaviors of *guai* (well behaved) and *Ting hua* (listening to adults' words), which are the most commonly used words to praise children in China. The emphasis on self-control in Chinese children is also related to the belief that human behavior is malleable and controllable – with adequate training, children can learn self-control skills and behave according to social expectations (Chen, 2010). Cultural values of self-control are reflected in organizing daily parent–child activities (e.g., feeding, sleeping, toilet training, teaching children not to grab toys from others, setting rules for children) from early childhood. Chen et al. (2003) found, for example, that whereas most Canadian children, particularly boys, wore diapers at the age of two, virtually all Chinese toddlers had finished toilet training by then. Many Chinese parents and grandparents indicated during interviews that they started toilet training when their children were under one year old.

Cross-cultural research has shown that relative to Western children, Chinese children display higher levels of self-control and related behaviors, such as persistence and diligence (e.g., Chen et al., 2003; Ding et al., 2021; Gartstein et al., 2006; Schirmbeck et al., 2020). For example, infants in China were rated by their mothers as higher than infants in Spain and the United States on duration of orienting (attention to and interaction with an object for extended periods of time) and soothability (reduced fussiness and distress when soothed by the caregiver) (Gartstein et al., 2006). When preschool-age children in China and the United States were presented with a piece of paper covered with randomly sequenced images of dogs, balls, and cups, and were asked to circle as many ball–dog pairs with the dog after the ball as they could in three minutes, Chinese children performed more competently than their US counterparts (Lan et al., 2011; Schirmbeck et al., 2020). Chen et al. (2003) found in an observational study that, compared with Canadian toddlers, Chinese toddlers waited longer on a delay task when they were told to wait to play with a packet of attractive crayons. During a clean-up session, Chinese toddlers also displayed a higher level of behavioral control than Canadian toddlers in completing the task without adult intervention.

Researchers in China have been interested in the role of self-control in child development as a mediator of parental socialization effort and a moderator of the negative effects of adverse life experiences. Ding et al. (2017) found that, through reducing deviant peer affiliation, self-control mediated the links between parental monitoring and decreased internet addiction. Liu and Chang (2016) examined in Taiwan how parental behavioral control (e.g., "When I do something wrong, father/mother will correct and guide me") was related to adolescents' obedience (the extent of obeying parental demands regarding daily rules such as "using pocket money" and "cleaning own room"). The relations were mediated by adolescents' intentional self-control (e.g., "I concentrate all my energy on a few things").

Self-control is believed to be particularly important for adaptive development of children in adverse circumstances (Zhao et al., 2016). For example, children who are left in the rural hometown by their parents who work in a city tend to display extensive adjustment difficulties, including feelings of insecurity, loneliness, and poor academic performance (Shen et al., 2015). In a study of problem behaviors in left-behind and nonleft-behind children in a rural region in China, Lei et al. (2019) found that left-behind children were more likely to be affiliated with deviant peers and display problem behaviors. However, self-control moderated the relations; those with a higher level of self-control displayed fewer problems. Moreover, the moderating effects were more evident in left-behind children than in nonleft-behind children.

The cultural values of self-control in Chinese society may promote its significance for development. Whereas self-control helps children perform in social and academic areas across cultures (e.g., Eisenberg et al., 2006), it appears to be related to adjustment more strongly and in broader domains in Chinese children than in Western children. Zhou et al. (2009), for example, found that self-control was more strongly associated with fewer externalizing behavioral problems in Chinese children than in US children. Self-control is consistently and negatively associated with internalizing problems, such as anxiety and depression, in Chinese children, suggesting that children high on self-control have fewer internalizing problems in China (Chen et al., 2012; Eisenberg et al., 2007; Muhtadie et al., 2013). However, the same associations in US children appear to be weak and mixed (e.g., children high on self-control report more internalizing problems; Murray & Kochanska, 2002; Volbrecht & Goldsmith, 2010). In short, given the great emphasis on self-control in China, children who fail to control their behaviors are likely to receive negative social evaluations in social interactions, which may enhance the development of externalizing as well as internalizing symptoms (Muhtadie et al., 2013).

Cheung and Park (2010) argued that adequate, but not excessive, control of individual emotions and behaviors may serve a self-protective function in individualistic cultures, but help individuals to better engage in prosocial and cooperative activities in collectivistic cultures. In other words, although self-control is generally useful for performance on social and cognitive tasks, specific developmental outcomes that self-control leads to may vary in different societies according to cultural socialization goals (e.g., personal versus group goals). In Western societies where individuality and autonomy are the major socialization goals, self-control may mostly serve to promote the development of independent skills and a sense of mastery and self-actualization. In Chinese society, however, the role of self-control may be manifested mainly in its contributions to the development of social behaviors, such as prosocial and cooperative behaviors, that are conductive to group functioning.

6 Social Behaviors in Childhood and Adolescence

Early dispositional characteristics (e.g., reactivity, self-control), culturally directed socialization attitudes and practices, and their interactions determine, to a large extent, the development of social behaviors. This section discusses three major social behaviors – prosocial behavior, aggression, and shyness – in Chinese children and adolescents. The discussion focuses on issues related to the cultural meanings, features, prevalence, and developmental outcomes of these behaviors.

6.1 Prosocial Behavior

Prosocial behavior, as voluntary behavior intended to benefit others (Eisenberg et al., 2015), is highly valued in collectivistic Chinese society because of its obvious benefits for social interaction and group functioning. Traditional Confucianism considers prosocial behavior a major component of virtuous character that should be deliberately cultivated during socialization. According to Mencius, human virtuous character is rooted in four predispositions or inborn qualities that he described as "sprouts": a feeling of compassion, a sense of shame, a reverential attitude toward others, and a sense of right and wrong. The four dispositions form the foundation for four major attributes of the ideal personality: *ren* (benevolence, humanity), *yi* (righteousness), *li* (propriety, proper conduct), and *zhi* (wisdom and knowledge). Mencius particularly emphasized compassion as an origin of *ren* (恻隐之心, 仁之端也), which is closely related to prosocial attitudes and behaviors. However, the innate tendency of compassion in the early years needs to be expanded and cultivated (扩而充之) through proper socialization and education so it can develop into prosocial attributes in childhood and adulthood.

6.1.1 Meanings of Prosocial Behavior

In Western cultures, it is believed that prosocial behavior should be a mostly spontaneous act without external pressure, derived from personal decision based on a consideration of balance between concern for others and individual choice or self-interest (Miller et al., 2018). In contrast, non-Western group-oriented cultures emphasize prosocial behavior as interpersonal obligation or social responsibility in response to the needs of others (Köster et al., 2015; Miller et al., 2018). There is evidence that, whereas providing support for individual autonomy helps children develop prosocial behavior in Western societies, encouragement of social responsibility and compliance with social norms is more effective in promoting children's prosocial behavior in group-oriented societies (Köster et al., 2015; Song et al., 2021). Consistent with the cross-cultural literature (e.g., Köster et al., 2015), research with Chinese children and adolescents has revealed that prosocial behavior is often interpreted and appreciated in the context of social relationships and group activities.

In several studies concerning the understanding of prosocial behavior using interviews, Kou and colleagues (Kou & Zhang, 2006; Yang et al., 2016) learned that Chinese children and adolescents viewed helping, sharing, cooperating, and comforting as typical indicators of prosocial behavior, which is consistent with the Western literature (e.g., Eisenberg et al., 2015). The similar perceptions in Chinese and Western children and adolescents may indicate the cross-culturally common features of prosocial behavior. In addition to the typical indicators, Chinese children and adolescents listed a number of behaviors and characteristics as prosocial that have been traditionally valued in Chinese culture, such as family responsibility, intimate relationships, modesty, being considerate of others, loyalty and faithfulness to friends, following social standards, gratitude, group orientation, and contribution to public welfare (Kou & Zhang, 2006).

Kou et al. (2007) conducted a more comprehensive study about the conceptual representation of prosocial behavior in Chinese adolescents. The analysis identified a four-dimension structure of altruism (e.g., helping classmates with homework, buying learning material for classmates from poor families), common-weal and social rule (e.g., obeying social order, respecting the old and loving the young), relationship (e.g., accepting others, intervening when others are fighting/arguing, playing with children who are lonely), and personal trait (e.g., modesty, politeness) (Kou et al., 2007). Many of the specific examples of prosocial behavior provided by children are related to how the actions benefit group interests and collective well-being, such as actively participating in activities organized by the school, shoveling snow off the walkway in front of the classroom, doing housework and helping other people in the family, and helping others to maintain harmonious relationships in the neighborhood (Kou et al., 2004). The broad view of prosocial behavior may allow Chinese children and adolescents to be sensitive to social-contextual circumstances in the judgment and display of the behavior.

6.1.2 Social-Contextual Features of Prosocial Behavior

Relative to their Western counterparts, Chinese children and adolescents are more sensitive to social circumstances and less sensitive to personal characteristics in the display of prosocial behavior (Kuang et al., 2021), which is consistent with Miller's argument (2018) that prosocial behavior is often regarded as indicating interpersonal obligation or social responsibility in collectivistic societies. In a study of emotional and behavioral reactions of college students to situations involving a single sick child or a group of sick children, for example, Wang, Tang, et al. (2015) found that participants in the United States displayed higher levels of sympathy and willingness to help an identified victim (the age, name, and picture of the victim were provided) than a victim without the personal information. In contrast, participants in China displayed higher levels of distress and sympathy and willingness to help a group of sick children than a single child, regardless of the personal identification information. Wang, Tang, et al. (2015) argued that, unlike the rights-based ethics of Western individualism, the ethics of Confucian relationalism emphasizes social situations in eliciting prosocial responding based on interpersonal duties. According to the authors, the results are also related to the influence of the moral ideal advocated by Mencius in Chinese culture – "Care for one's own aged parents and extend the same care to all aged parents; love one's own young children and extend the same love to all young children (老吾老, 以及人之老; 幼吾幼, 以及人之幼)."

Kuang et al. (2021) conducted a study of resource sharing in urban and rural Chinese children. Children were asked to imagine that they and another child won 100 yuan in a lottery. Then, the children were asked to decide how much they want to keep and how much (if any) they want to give to the partner. Western children and adults tend to share more to more needy recipients (e.g., children who did not have toys) or to lower-class targets (Malti et al., 2016; Van Doesum et al., 2017). The results are often explained from a fairness perspective – individuals with limited resources may receive more prosocial behavior as a compensation (Van Doesum et al., 2017). To link this perspective to understanding prosocial behavior in the Chinese urban–rural context, Kuang et al. (2021) asked the children to share with a partner from a rural, urban, or unspecified background. In general, children provided more offers to a rural partner than to an urban partner or a partner of unspecified background. Moreover, the offers to rural partners by urban children were higher than those offered by rural children. Similar results were found in Chen et al.'s study (2019), which indicated that, compared with their urban nonmigrant counterparts, rural-to-urban migrant children were more accepted and received greater support from peers in Shanghai. Whereas these results might be in line with the fairness perspective (Van Doesum et al., 2017), they were interpreted mainly in terms of children's understanding of the relatively adverse life circumstances of families in rural regions and display of helping behavior as a social obligation or a response to social requirements in the context of China's dual urban–rural structure (Kuang et al., 2021).

6.1.3 Prevalence of Prosocial Behavior

Chinese children tend to display more prosocial behaviors, such as sharing, than their counterparts in Western countries. Kuang et al.'s study (2021) reported that, on average, the offers to the recipients were over 50 percent (and 70 percent to rural children by the urban children) of the total amount of the resources, which was significantly higher than the proportions reported in studies with Western samples. Willingness to share in Chinese children was examined more systematically by Rao and Stewart (1999). In their study, a sample of four-year-old kindergarten Chinese children in Hong Kong was observed in a semi-naturalistic situation. To assess sharing behaviors, one child (sharer) was given ten pieces of his/her preferred food and ten pieces of his/her least preferred food (e.g., potato chips, chocolate buttons, bite-size crackers, carrots), whereas another child (either a friend or an acquaintance as the partner or recipient) was given one piece of each of the same foods. Sharing behaviors were coded to indicate whether they were initiated by the sharer (spontaneous sharing) or due to the recipients' requests (elicited sharing). The researchers examined sharing behaviors in Chinese children in comparison with the results from a sample of US children using the same procedure. The analysis first showed that Chinese children were more likely to share and displayed more spontaneous sharing than US children. When the partner elicited sharing, Chinese children were less likely than US children to resist sharing. Moreover, whereas US children were more likely to share with friends than nonfriends, Chinese children shared equally with friends and nonfriends. Rao and Stewart (1999) argued that the cross-cultural differences might be due to the greater emphasis on social relatedness and group goals in Chinese society, which supports the encouragement of helping each other and sharing scarce resources in childrearing and education.

The willingness of Chinese children to share has been found in other studies concerning general prosocial and cooperative behaviors in naturalistic settings. Navon and Ramsey (1989), for example, observed three- to four-year-old children's free play activities during periods when there was little involvement of teachers in a daycare center in Nanjing, China. They coded observations using a scheme that included prosocial behaviors, such as sharing toys, redistributing materials (e.g., toys) among all the children, and assisting in cleaning up material. Compared with their counterparts in the United States, Chinese children displayed a significantly higher level of sharing and other prosocial behaviors. For example, sharing occurred in 11 percent of the total behaviors in Chinese children but only 5 percent of the total behaviors in US children. Approximately 14 percent of the behaviors in Chinese children were about redistribution of materials; children often voluntarily distributed materials to another child when they noticed that he/she did not have the materials. In contrast, no such distributing behaviors were observed in the US sample; they were never seen to spontaneously give away materials that was in their possession. When a peer took a toy of a child, US children engaged in disputes nearly three times as often as did the Chinese children. In almost half of the taking episodes (43 percent) in which a peer removed a toy from their pile, Chinese children exhibited no obvious reaction. However, "no reaction" never occurred in these episodes in US children.

In a similar study, Orlick et al. (1990) conducted naturalistic observations in three kindergartens in Beijing, China, and three kindergartens in Ottawa, Canada. Children's prosocial behaviors were coded for those involving sharing, helping, or physical affection. The study revealed remarkable differences between Chinese and Canadian children. Of the social behaviors displayed by the children, 85 percent were prosocial in China, whereas only 22 percent were prosocial in Canada. Orlick et al. (1990) argued that, in addition to greater emphasis placed on helping and sharing in Chinese kindergartens, practices in kindergarten education might play a role, such as organizing play activities to facilitate cooperative interactions, reading stories about group activities in children's books, and using peer role models in the class to promote prosocial behavior.

Among the factors that may explain the relatively high levels of sharing, helping, and other prosocial behaviors in Chinese children, collectivistic values, such as group orientation and other orientation, have been emphasized in the literature (Kuang et al., 2021; Rao & Stewart, 1999; Stewart & McBride-Chang, 2000). Zhou et al. (2022) assessed parental collectivistic childrearing goals (e.g., "My parents want me to have harmonious relationships with people around me") and examined their relations with prosocial behavior in a sample of Chinese adolescents. Collectivistic goals positively contributed to adolescents' prosocial behavior one year later. Liu, Fu, et al. (2018) examined relations between self-reported group orientation (e.g., "It is important to me to respect decisions made by the group") and teacher-rated social competence, which included prosocial attitudes and behaviors, among children in urban and rural regions of China. Group orientation was associated with social competence in rural, but not urban, children, suggesting that group-oriented values are likely to have more evident effects on individual behaviors when the values are more endorsed in the community.

According to Navon and Ramsey (1989), children's sharing behavior is related to their awareness of, and attitudes toward, individual ownership and private property. The increased abundance of personal goods, for example, may lead to a greater sense of individual ownership and need for protection of private property (e.g., "This is mine/his/hers" as opposed to "This belongs to all of us"), which, in turn, may reduce perceived social responsibility to display prosocial behavior toward others. If this is the case, the social changes in China due to reforms from the centrally planned command economy, with the dominance of state-owned enterprises, to a market economy that is characterized by the rapid growth of private enterprises, may have an impact on people's attitudes about individual ownership and private property. In a study of children's views about private versus public property, Chen, Li, et al. (2018) examined judgments of damage to private versus public property among elementary school students (seven to eleven years) in China at two historical times (1980 and 2012). In the study, the children were administered paired stories that described a protagonist who damaged private property (e.g., another child's backpack or clothes) or public property (classroom curtains or flowers in the school garden). Children in the 2012 cohort were more likely than their counterparts in the 1980 cohort to judge damage to private property as more culpable than damage to public property. The cohort differences were more evident in older children than in younger children. It remains to be examined whether greater appreciation of personal private property and stronger beliefs about individual rights and protection of self-interest result in reduced sharing and other prosocial behaviors in Chinese children.

6.1.4 Prosocial Behavior and Social, School, and Psychological Adjustment

Given its potential benefits for others, prosocial behavior is conceivably associated with positive social responses and positive adjustment among children across cultures (e.g., Eisenberg et al., 2015). Indeed, children who display prosocial behavior are liked by peers, obtain a high status in the peer group, and perform well on school tasks (Eisenberg et al., 2015). The mechanisms underlying relations between prosocial behavior and social and school adjustment involve social-relational and social-cognitive processes. Specifically, prosocial behavior helps create an environment which provides increased opportunities for children to learn skills and receive assistance from others. Moreover, the regulatory abilities that prosocial children possess help them understand social norms and expectations, maintain their effort to concentrate on tasks, and control their disruptive and deviant behaviors in social interactions, which, in turn, help them achieve success.

Consistent with the literature (Eisenberg et al., 2015), research with Chinese children has indicated robust links between prosocial behavior and social and school adjustment (e.g., Chen, 2010). Chen, Li, et al. (2000), for example, found in a two-year longitudinal study that peer-assessed prosocial behavior (e.g., "Helps others when they need it," "Considerate of others") made significant contributions to later peer acceptance, leadership status, and academic achievement in Chinese children. A follow-up study showed that prosocial behavior at twelve years positively predicted educational attainment, supportive peer relationships, and active involvement in constructive activities, such as art and dance, sports, literature, and science, seven years later (Chen et al., 2002). In addition, Chen et al., (2019) found that Chinese adolescents' prosocial behavior negatively predicted later substance use (using tobacco, using alcohol, and getting drunk) and deviant behavior (e.g., skipping classes, going to places parents do not approve). Taken together, the existing findings based on children and adolescents in China clearly demonstrate that prosocial behavior positively contributes to the attainment of social status and academic achievement and negatively contributes to the development of behavioral problems, particularly of an externalizing nature.

That said, relations between prosocial behavior and internalizing problems are less clear in Chinese children. Chen, Li, et al. (2000) and Chen et al. (2002) showed that prosocial behavior was positively correlated with perceived self-worth and negatively with loneliness and depression. However, after its overlap with sociability, which indicated the tendency to initiate and maintain social interactions and relationships (e.g., "Likes to play with others rather than alone"), was controlled, prosocial behavior did not significantly predict self-worth or internalizing problems. Jin et al. (2021) examined relations among prosocial behavior, peer relationships, and depression in a multi-wave longitudinal study with panel data collected each year from Grade 3 to Grade 6 in a sample of elementary school children in China. Prosocial behavior and depression negatively contributed to each other over time when peer preference was not included in the model. However, the direct reciprocal contributions of prosocial behavior and depression became nonsignificant when peer preference was included. Instead, prosocial behavior predicted increased peer preference, which, in turn, predicted fewer depressive symptoms. Thus, prosocial behavior contributed to reduced depressive symptoms through the mediation of peer preference. It has been argued that prosocial behavior may be linked with psychological well-being through internal processes, such as self-regulation of negative emotions (Eisenberg et al., 2015). The research findings based on Chinese children suggest that prosocial behavior helps attain psychological well-being and reduces internalizing problems mainly through the mediation of active social participation and positive peer relationships. Provisions of social support and interpersonal connectedness may be necessary for the operation of internal processes in the contributions of prosocial behavior to psychological adjustment.

6.2 Aggressive Behavior

Whereas prosocial behavior represents an individual tendency to get along with others, aggressive behavior, defined as the "behavior through which individuals intentionally cause physical or psychological harm to others" (Eisner & Malti, 2015, p. 795), is largely concerned with an individual tendency to move against others. Aggressive behavior is discouraged in most cultures because of its potential harm to the well-being of others and the group. In societies that place greater emphasis on social harmony, aggressive behavior is likely viewed as more deviant and thus evaluated more negatively by adults and peers (Bergeron & Schneider, 2005). As a result, aggressive children in these societies, including China, may experience heightened difficulties in social interaction and adjustment.

6.2.1 Parental and Peer Attitudes toward Aggressive Behavior

From evolutionary and social control perspectives (e.g., Bond, 2004; Vaughn & Santos, 2007), aggressive behavior has adaptive value for acquiring resources and promoting social status and power. According to bi-strategic resource control theory (Hawley & Bower, 2018), aggressive behavior may be an effective strategy, along with prosocial behavior, to gain social dominance (attention, prestige, status) in interactions with others, particularly in a hierarchically organized society with limited resources. Consistent with theory, research in Western countries indicates that whereas, in general, aggressive children are likely to display problems in social relationships and school adjustment, such as peer rejection and learning problems (Eisner & Malti, 2015), they may receive support and be regarded as popular or even "stars" in their groups (e.g., Rodkin et al., 2000; Wurster & Xie, 2014).

In Chinese society, aggressive behavior is viewed as in discord with group-oriented values. The cultural sanction against aggressive behavior has been found with Chinese children and adolescents. Greenberger et al. (2000) conducted a cross-cultural study concerning adolescent-reported parental attitudes ("would not care," "would be somewhat upset," and "would be very upset") and close friend's attitudes ("approve," "say nothing," and "disapproval") toward misconduct, including aggressive behavior. Students in senior high schools in China and South Korea had higher scores on perceived sanctions of parents and close friends than did their counterparts in the United States. Compared with US adolescents, Chinese and Korean adolescents believed that their parents and friends were less tolerant or approving of aggressive behavior. Chinese adolescents also perceived friends as more disapproving of aggressive behavior than did Korean adolescents.

In a separate study focusing on peer attitudes toward misconduct, Chen, Greenberger, et al. (1998) assessed adolescents' perceptions of peer approval and disapproval of aggressive behavior and other antisocial behaviors among students in middle schools in Beijing, Taipei, and the United States. Chinese adolescents in Beijing and Taipei had significantly lower scores on peer approval for the behaviors than did European American adolescents. Chinese American adolescents fell between the two Chinese groups and the European American group. Moreover, Chinese adolescents in Beijing and Taipei reported a higher level of peer disapproval of the behaviors than did European and Chinese American adolescents. Taken together, these results indicate that Chinese adolescents are less likely than US adolescents to believe that their peers and parents would endorse aggressive behavior. The results also suggest that adolescents in the more traditional Chinese society (e.g., Beijing) tend to perceive a higher level of disapproval of aggressive behavior than adolescents in more industrialized or Westernized societies (e.g., Taiwan and Seoul; Greenberger et al., 2000). Similarly, in a study about social attitudes toward bullying behavior, Ji et al. (2016) found that, compared with their counterparts in England, elementary and middle school students in China displayed more negative attitudes toward bullying behavior and a greater willingness to act to stop bullying. The different attitudes in Chinese and English students were more evident in the higher grades.

Negative social attitudes of parents and peers toward children's aggression have also emerged in studies of its relations with parent–child and peer relationships. Chen, Rubin, and Li (1997), for example, examined relations between aggressive behavior and maternal acceptance in a sample of Chinese children at eight and ten years of age. Aggressive behavior was assessed using peer evaluations (e.g., "Someone who gets into a lot of fights," "Someone who picks on other kids"), and maternal acceptance and rejection were assessed using mothers' reports (e.g., "My child and I have warm, intimate times together," "I enjoy having my child around me," "I often feel angry with my child"). Child aggression was negatively associated with maternal acceptance and positively associated with maternal rejection. The analysis of four-year longitudinal data revealed that child aggression and maternal acceptance and rejection contributed to each other in a reciprocal manner. Chen, Liu, et al. (2000) further examined relations between adolescent-reported parental warmth ("My father/mother makes me feel better after talking over my worries," "Enjoys doing things with me," "Says I am a big problem") and social behaviors and psychological adjustment in China. Whereas maternal warmth was positively associated with psychological adjustment, such as feelings of loneliness and depression, paternal warmth was negatively associated with adolescent aggression. In the Chinese family, the mother is more likely to engage in affective communications with children and provide emotional support to them, whereas the role of the father, as the authority figure, is mainly to help children learn social values and display socially appropriate behaviors, particularly from late childhood to adolescence. "To feed without teaching, is the father's fault," as stated in the famous *Three-Character Classic* (Cambridge Chinese Classics, 2022). Therefore, fathers may be more likely than mothers to feel responsible for and display negative reactions to children's aggressive behavior.

He et al. (2019) examined relations between adolescent aggression and parental psychological control in a sample of middle school students in Beijing. Adolescent aggressive behavior significantly and positively contributed to later parental guilt induction (e.g., "My parents tell me that I should feel guilty when I do not meet their expectations"), love withdrawal (e.g., "My parents act cold and unfriendly if I do something they do not like"), and authority assertion (e.g., "My parents tell me that what they want me to do is the best for me and I should not question it"). The contributions were consistent for boys and girls.

Gao et al. (2015) explored how child aggression was associated with the indigenous parenting style of *guan* in a sample of elementary and middle school students in Hong Kong. Parents were asked to complete measures of child reactive aggression (e.g., "reacted angrily when provoked by others"), proactive aggression (e.g., "hurts others to win a game"), and *guan* (e.g., "I emphasized self-discipline," "I pointed out good behaviors in others as a model for my child"). Whereas proactive aggression was negatively associated with *guan*, reactive aggression was positively associated with *guan*, suggesting that parents might have different attitudes toward the two types of aggression. Similarly, Xu et al. (2009b) found different relations between parental attitudes and types of aggression; although both proactive aggression and reactive aggression were positively associated with harsh parental attitudes (e.g., use physical punishment as a way of disciplining our child, yell or shout when child misbehaves), the relation was stronger for reactive aggression than for proactive aggression. A major difference between proactive aggression and reactive aggression is that the latter is more likely to be "hotheaded," derived from frustration, anger, and emotional outbursts (Xu et al., 2009b). The more negative parental reaction to children's reactive aggression in Chinese parents may be related to the cultural emphasis on self-control.

A large number of studies has examined relations between aggression and peer acceptance and rejection in Chinese children and adolescents (e.g., Chen et al., 1992, 2005; Xu & Zhang, 2008). Aggressive behavior is positively associated with peer rejection and negatively associated with peer acceptance. However, the magnitudes of the associations appear to differ in Chinese and Western, particularly North American, samples. The relations between aggression and peer rejection, indexed by negative sociometric nominations (e.g., "Someone you would not like to be/play/work with"), are typically about 0.70 in Chinese children (e.g., Chen et al., 1995, 2005). The magnitudes of these relations tend to be lower in adolescents (e.g., $r = 0.50$s, Wang, Zhang, et al., 2015), indicating that as the desire for individual autonomy becomes stronger with age, aggressive behavior may be more likely to be perceived as cool and assertive (Rodkin et al., 2000). Similar results about relations between aggression and peer rejection have been found in Chinese children and adolescents in different parts of Chinese society, including mainland China, Hong Kong, and Taiwan. Tseng et al. (2013), for example, found in a sample of fifth grade students in Taiwan that physical aggression, as assessed using peer nominations, was positively correlated with peer rejection (rs = 0.56 and 0.65, respectively). These relations using the same method are often weaker (e.g., correlations between aggression and peer preference range from −0.20s to −0.50s in middle to late childhood) in Western children at similar ages (e.g., Zimmer-Gembeck et al., 2005; van den Berg et al., 2015). Moreover, Chen, He, et al. (2004) found that aggression was significantly and negatively associated with the possession of mutual friendship in Chinese, Brazilian, and Italian children (rs = −0.17, −0.10, and -0.12, ps < 0.001, 0.01, and 0.01, respectively), but the association was not significant in Canadian children (r = −0.04, p > 0.05). Along with these results, Chen and Tse (2008) found in a sample of elementary school students in Canada that aggression was positively associated with victimization more strongly in Chinese Canadian children than in European Canadian children.

In a cross-cultural study with seven-year-olds in China and Canada (French et al., 2011), groups of four children who were unfamiliar with each other were invited to the university laboratory and administered a limited resources play session in which the researcher placed a single attractive toy in the room. Upon completion of the session, the children were individually interviewed about how much they liked playing with the other children in the group. Different patterns of the relations between children's behaviors and peer likability were found in the two groups. Specifically, children who used aggressive and other assertive behaviors to gain the toy (e.g., grabbing the toy from another child) were more liked by their peers in Canada but less liked by their peers in China. In contrast, children who displayed passive behavior to obtain the toy (e.g., weak or indirect attempts to obtain control of the toy, such as approaching or moving toward the child with the toy) and let others play with the toy were more liked by their peers in China but less liked by their peers in Canada. Thus, relative to Canadian children, Chinese children were more likely to prefer nonaggressive, passive behavior in situations involving limited resources and potential conflict.

In sum, researchers have studied social attitudes toward aggressive behavior in China using different methods, such as assessing children's and adolescents' views (e.g., Greenberger et al., 2000) and analyzing relations between aggression and social acceptance and rejection (e.g., Chen, He, et al., 2004; French et al., 2011; Wang, Zhang, et al., 2015). The results suggest that aggressive behavior is associated with more negative parental and peer attitudes in Chinese children than in Western children. These results are consistent with the literature showing the general patterns of variations across societies in parental and peer endorsement of aggressive behavior as a function of cultural values of group harmony and conformity to social standards (e.g., Bergeron & Schneider, 2005; Bond, 2004; Greenfield et al., 2006; Lansford et al., 2018).

6.2.2 Prevalence of Aggressive Behavior

In a comprehensive review of aggressive behavior, Bergeron and Schneider (2005) found that, in cultures that are characterized by collectivistic values, particularly Confucian values of group orientation and high moral discipline, individuals display lower levels of aggression than their counterparts in individualistic cultures. Lansford et al. (2018) also found that, in cultures in which parents expressed lower endorsement of aggression, school-age children displayed less aggressive and other externalizing behaviors. Relatively little research has been conducted to directly compare children in China and other countries on aggressive behavior, perhaps due to difficulties in maintaining cross-cultural equivalence in the assessment of aggression (Putnick & Bornstein, 2016). Nevertheless, results from existing studies appear to indicate that, consistent with the findings of Bergeron and Schneider (2005) and Lansford et al. (2018), Chinese children tend to display less aggressive behavior than children in Western countries.

In one of the first cross-cultural studies about adolescents' aggression, Crystal et al. (1994) examined aggressive behavior among high school students in Taiwan, Japan, and the United States. The participants reported their aggression on items like "In the past month, how often have you: (a) felt like hitting someone, (b) felt like destroying something, (c) gotten into serious arguments or fights with other students, (d) felt angry at your teacher?" using a 5-point scale ranging from 1 ("never") to 5 ("almost every day"). Adolescents in Taiwan and Japan had lower scores on reported feelings of aggression than their counterparts in the Unites States. Jessor et al. (2003) asked high school students in China and the United States to report on problem behaviors, including physical aggression, and found that Chinese students, especially girls, reported lower levels of aggression than US students. Using a similar approach, Greenberger et al. (2000) asked adolescents in China, South Korea, and the United States to report their involvement in aggressive and other problem behaviors. Chinese adolescents had lower scores than both Korean and US adolescents. The proportion of Chinese adolescents who engaged in aggressive acts was substantially lower than the proportions of Korean and US adolescents. For example, 11 percent of Chinese adolescents, 18 percent of Korean adolescents, and 52 percent of US adolescents reportedly "hit or threatened to hit someone." Chinese and Korean adolescents reported less aggressive and other externalizing behaviors among family members, friends, and school peers than did US adolescents. Chinese adolescents also reported less aggressive behaviors among family members, friends, and school peers than did Korean adolescents. According to Greenberger et al. (2000), the more aggressive behaviors reported by Korean adolescents than by Chinese adolescents may be because Korean adolescents were exposed to more Western individualistic values and lifestyles than were Chinese adolescents.

Lansford et al. (2012) compared elementary school children (ages seven to ten years) in nine countries (China, Colombia, Italy, Jordan, Kenya, the Philippines, Sweden, Thailand, and the United States) on physical and relational aggression. Children were asked how often in the last thirty days they engaged in aggressive acts that were physical (throwing something at someone to hurt them, shoving or pushing, and hitting or slapping other children) and relational (excluding another child from a group, trying to keep others from liking someone by saying mean things about that person, and saying things about another child to make people laugh). Children in China and Thailand had lower scores on physical aggression than their counterparts in the other countries. Also, children in China, Italy, and Thailand reported being more relationally than physically aggressive. In contrast, children in Jordan and Kenya reported being more physically than relationally aggressive, and no significant differences between physical aggression and relational aggression were reported by children in other countries. As Lansford et al. (2012) explained, children may use a particular type of aggression in a culture according to their judgments of the risks and benefits associated with that type of aggression. The relatively higher levels of relational aggression reported by children in China, Italy, and Thailand may be due to their perceptions of lower risks of using relational aggression (e.g., they are less likely to be punished for relationally aggressive acts than for physically aggressive acts). It should be noted that this explanation is different from the argument made by Kawabata and Crick (2013) that relational aggression is regarded as more harmful to social relationships and group well-being and thus is more likely to lead to adults' disapproval and peer rejection in group-oriented, particularly East Asian, societies.

Chen and Tse (2008) conducted a study of social behaviors in several public elementary schools in Canada. The sample consisted of Canadian-born children with Chinese and European backgrounds. Children's aggression was assessed using a peer-nomination measure. Compared with European Canadian children, Chinese Canadian children were viewed as less aggressive by students not only in the Chinese group but also in European and other ethnic groups (e.g., non-Chinese Asian, Latinos). According to Chen and Tse (2008), the socialization experiences of Chinese Canadian children at home, such as parental encouragement of behavioral control, may help them learn to constrain their aggressive and disruptive behaviors in social settings.

6.2.3 Aggressive Behavior and Adjustment

Aggressive behavior is generally associated with negative developmental outcomes, such as low social status and poor academic performance, in children and adolescents across cultures (Chen et al., 2005; Lansford et al., 2018). Despite the general pattern, there is evidence that in cultures with stronger sanctions against aggression, aggressive children may receive more negative social evaluations, which in turn contribute to more maladaptive development. For example, aggressive children in North America tend to develop inflated self-perceptions of social competence and typically do not report internalizing psychological problems (Chen, He, et al., 2004; Rubin et al., 1995). However, aggressive children in China often develop pervasive adjustment problems, including negative self-perceptions, depression, and loneliness (Chen, 2010).

Chen, He, et al. (2004) examined relations between aggression and loneliness among elementary school children in China, Brazil, Canada, and Italy. Aggression was positively associated with loneliness in China and Italy, but not in Brazil and Canada. Moreover, aggression significantly contributed to loneliness through the mediation of negative peer relationships (low peer preference and lack of friendship) in Chinese children, whereas the contributions were not significant in the other samples. Xu and Zhang (2008) found in Chinese elementary school children that proactive aggression and reactive aggression were positively associated with loneliness and social anxiety although the relation between reactive aggression and psychological problems was more evident. Consistent with these results, a meta-analysis indicated that, whereas mixed relations were found between aggression and self-esteem in Western children and adolescents, virtually all types of aggression (physical aggression, anger, hostility, implicit and explicit aggression) were associated with low self-esteem in Chinese students (Teng et al., 2015). The negative self-perceptions and low self-esteem of Chinese aggressive students may be related to the public social evaluations in the school, in which students collectively evaluate each other in terms of whether they behave appropriately and whether they reach the school standards (Chen, 2010). The negative feedback that aggressive children receive from others makes it difficult for them to overestimate their social competence and develop positive self-perceptions and self-feelings.

Researchers have examined the adjustment outcomes of relational aggression in Chinese children (e.g., Kawabata et al., 2012; Kawabata & Crick, 2013; Tseng et al., 2013). Relational aggression is a form of aggression that is used to damage another child's social relationships, such as social exclusion, spreading rumors, and threatening to end friendships (Crick & Grotpeter, 1995). In Western societies, whereas relationally aggressive children are disliked by peers and display psychological problems, such as depression (e.g., Crick & Grotpeter, 1995), they may also be perceived as socially skilled and popular in school (LaFontana & Cillessen, 2002; Rose et al., 2004). Relational aggression is regarded as more harmful in East Asian collectivistic societies as it may disrupt interpersonal relationships and group harmony (Tseng et al., 2013). Kawabata et al. (2012) conducted a longitudinal study in Chinese students examining the development of relational aggression. Relational aggression increased with age in girls and but not in boys. Whereas both relational and physical aggressions predicted increases in depression and anxiety, the effect size for relational aggression was larger than that for physical aggression.

Kawabata and Crick (2013) further examined associations of relational aggression and physical aggression with teacher-rated externalizing and internalizing problems in Chinese and other Asian American children and European American children in the United States. Compared with European American children, Asian American children displayed lower levels of relational and physical aggression. Moreover, the associations between relational aggression and internalizing adjustment problems were stronger in Asian American children than in European American children.

In brief, children's aggressive behavior may elicit highly negative social evaluations in the group-oriented Chinese society. The unfavorable social experience of aggressive children renders them at heightened risk for developing social, behavioral, and school adjustment problems. Moreover, the feedback that aggressive children receive from adults and peers on a regular basis may undermine their self-confidence and prevent them from developing positive self-perceptions and self-feelings, which in turn may lead to internalizing problems, such as loneliness and depression. Therefore, aggressive behavior is associated with wide-ranging maladaptive developmental outcomes in Chinese children.

6.3 Shyness

Virtually all major developmental theories, including cognitive development theory (Piaget, 1932), social learning theory (Bandura, 1977), and interpersonal psychodynamic theory (Sullivan, 1953), highlight the significance of social interactions as a main mechanism for human development. The primary functions of social interactions include (1) providing opportunities for children to learn skills to cooperate with others on problem-solving and to learn rules in the society for appropriate behaviors, (2) helping children develop self-identity through social interaction experiences, and (3) facilitating the formation of social relationships that are sources of emotional support for children to cope with challenges in adjustment (Hartup, 1996; Rubin et al., 2015). Given the importance of social interactions, it is understandable that children who display a low level of social participation and engage in little interaction with others are likely to be at a disadvantage in development. Thus, social withdrawal, representing the tendency to move away from others, has traditionally been considered a risk factor in developing social, cognitive, and psychological problems (Rubin et al., 2009). Findings from empirical studies have largely supported these arguments: social withdrawal is associated with, and predictive of, peer rejection or isolation, poor academic performance, and psychopathological symptoms in childhood and adolescence (Rubin et al., 2009).

Social withdrawal is defined as individual solitary behavior in social settings or staying alone when opportunities to interact with others are available (Rubin et al., 2009). Whereas the definition of social withdrawal is rather straightforward, its meanings, behavioral and emotional features, and consequences are highly complex, largely depending on the motivations underlying the behavior. Asendorpf (1990) proposed a theoretical model from a motivational perspective, delineating three types of social withdrawal: shyness, unsociability, and social avoidance. Shyness is derived from conflictual motivations of approach and avoidance and manifested as excessively wary, vigilant, and self-conscious behaviors in contexts of social novelty or perceived social evaluation. Shy children often demonstrate interest in social interaction. However, their approach motivation is hindered by a high level of fear and anxiety in challenging situations (Asendorpf, 1991). Unsociability, a term often used interchangeably with social disinterest and preference for solitude, is derived from a low motivation for social interaction. Unsociable children may not actively avoid peer interaction, but they lack a strong desire to play with others and prefer to engage in solitary activities when they have a choice (Coplan et al., 2013). Finally, social avoidance, based on the combination of low social approach and high social avoidance motivations, represents active evasion of social interactions with others (Asendorpf, 1990; Coplan & Armer, 2007). It has been suggested that socially avoidant children may have experienced repeated exposure to negative peer treatments and their avoidant behavior may be a manifestation of social anhedonia and depression (Coplan et al., 2018).

Among the types of social withdrawal, shyness has received the most attention for several reasons: (1) it is viewed as an indication of social incompetence or failure to achieve the goal for social interaction, (2) it is associated with negative emotions, such as fear and anxiety, and (3) it contributes to the development of social-relational, cognitive, and psychopathological problems (Rubin et al., 2009). Researchers have explored children's unsociability and social avoidance (Bowker & Raja, 2011; Coplan et al., 2019). However, relatively little is known about these two types of social withdrawal in terms of their developmental origins and outcomes.

Similarly, research on social withdrawal in Chinese children has focused on shyness. Shyness in Chinese children is an interesting issue partly because research indicates that Chinese children appear inclined to display shy, wary, and vigilant behaviors in social situations (Chen, 2019). As discussed in Section 5.1, based on parental ratings and observations (e.g., Ahadi et al., 1993; Chen et al., 1998), compared with Western children, Chinese children show a higher reactivity in stressful settings, which is a temperamental trait that predicts shyness (Rubin et al., 2009). Moreover, cross-cultural research has consistently shown that Chinese adolescents and adults report higher levels of shyness and related characteristics, such as social anxiety, than their counterparts in Western countries (Kong et al., 2022; Rapee et al., 2011; Zhong et al., 2021). Chen and Tse (2008) also found in public elementary schools in Canada that, among Canadian-born children, Chinese Canadians, particularly girls, had higher scores than European Canadians on shyness. Similarly, Huntsinger and Jose (2006) found that second-generation Chinese American youth reported higher levels of shyness than their European American counterparts. Given this background, a theoretically and practically important question is whether shy Chinese children display problems in social interactions and develop difficulties in social, academic, and psychological adjustment. From the contextual-developmental perspective (Chen, 2012, 2018), this question is related to how adults and peers perceive and evaluate shyness, which is determined, to a large extent, by cultural norms and values in Chinese society.

6.3.1 Parental and Peer Attitudes toward Shyness

Shyness due to internal fear, anxiety, and a lack of self-confidence is viewed as incompatible with the socialization goal to help children develop autonomy and social assertiveness in Western cultures (Greenfield et al., 2006). Moreover, because shy children have the desire to interact with others but are not able to do so, shyness is considered an indication of social failure and incompetence. Research in the West has shown that parents tend to regard shy children as socially immature and often express disappointment, frustration, and rejection toward them (e.g., Hane et al., 2008; Tani et al., 2014). When children display shy behavior in social settings, parents express concern and other negative emotions and attempt to use coercive strategies, such as direct command and reprimand, to help them reduce shy behavior (Chen et al., 1998; Rubin et al., 2009).

Shy children in China may not experience the external pressure as their Western counterparts do to change their behavior while coping with their internal anxiety in social situations. Assertive and self-expressive behaviors are not highly valued or encouraged in Chinese culture. Moreover, behavioral restraint that shy children display may be considered useful for the maintenance of group harmony. As such, shyness may be positively evaluated and accepted by others (Chen & French, 2008).

Chen, Rubin, and Li (1997) examined relations between maternal attitudes and shyness among school-age children in China. Shyness was positively associated with maternal acceptance (e.g., "I enjoy having my child around me") and negatively associated with maternal rejection (e.g., "I often feel angry with my child"). In a separate study, Chen, Dong, and Zhou (1997) found that shyness was negatively associated with high-power parenting attitudes (e.g., "I do not allow my child to question my decisions") in Chinese children. These results suggest that, unlike shy children in Western countries, shy children in China receive parental support.

Peer attitudes toward shyness also differ between Chinese and Western children. Shyness is typically associated with peer isolation and rejection in Western societies (Rubin et al., 2009). However, a series of studies conducted by Chen and colleagues in the early 1990s (e.g., Chen et al., 1992; Chen, Dong, & Zhou, 1997) revealed that shyness was associated with peer acceptance in Chinese children. Rapee et al. (2011) examined youth's attitudes toward shy behavior in East Asian (China, Japan, and South Korea) and Western (Australia, Canada, Germany, The Netherlands, and the United States) countries using hypothetical vignettes. The vignettes described shy and reserved behaviors and outgoing and socially confident behaviors (e.g., a male character is "often reserved and would rarely start a conversation with anyone. When he speaks up, he sometimes blushes a little bit and may look a little uncomfortable"). After each vignette was presented, the participants were asked how popular or liked the person would be and to what extent they believed the behaviors described in the vignette would help or hinder the character's future career (e.g., future career options, future relationships with colleagues, and future relationships with bosses). Whereas Western youth viewed outgoing behavior as more desirable than shy behavior, East Asian youth viewed outgoing and shy behaviors as less different, suggesting that youth in East Asian countries were more accepting of shy behavior than youth in Western countries. Moreover, East Asian youth believed that outgoing versus shy behaviors had a smaller impact on future careers than did Western youth.

Zhang and Xu (2019) argued that different peer attitudes toward shyness in Chinese and US children might be due to their implicit views about the nature of shyness. Individuals who hold an "entity view" believe that behavior is fixed and immutable in quality, and individuals who hold an "incremental view" believe that behavior is not fixed and changes over time and situations with effort (Dweck, 1999). According to Zhang and Xu (2019), peers with an entity view are inclined to make rigid stereotypical judgments of shy children based on limited information, whereas peers with an incremental view tend to make flexible interpersonal judgments that take different perspectives into consideration. The researchers examined implicit views of shyness in fourth and fifth grade students in China and the United States. Children were asked to indicate their agreement on items such as "Some children are shy and others are not. Nothing they do will change things," "Some children are shy and they will always be that way even when they grow up," "Some children can change their shyness if they want to," and "A child's shyness is not fixed, but changes over time." US children reported stronger entity views of shyness, whereas Chinese children reported stronger incremental views of shyness.

In addition to assessing implicit views, Zhang and Xu (2019) asked children to nominate classmates whom they thought were shy and then to report their relationships with the shy classmates by answering three questions: "How often do you play with . . .?" "Would you consider . . . not your friend?" and "How do you like . . .?" Chinese children were more likely than US children to be playmates or friends with shy classmates. Chinese children also liked their shy classmates more than US children did. Moreover, mediational analyses showed that culture (Chinese versus American) was associated with children's reported relationships with shy classmates through the mediation of implicit views, suggesting that relatively stronger entity views among US children partly explained why they reported worse relationships with shy classmates than their Chinese counterparts.

As a result of macro-level social, economic, and cultural changes, social attitudes toward shyness in Chinese children have become increasingly negative. In the new environment, behavioral qualities such as exploration and initiative-taking are required to achieve success and thus are gradually appreciated in the society (Cai et al., 2020). Social attitudes toward shyness seem to be particularly susceptible to the influence of the social and cultural changes because shyness clearly does not fit with the requirements of the competitive society.

Research conducted from the early 2000s provided evidence about negative parental attitudes toward children's shyness in urban China. Yan et al. (2016), for example, found in urban Chinese samples that children's shyness was negatively associated with parental support and positively associated with parental punitive parenting. Liu et al. (2018) found in a longitudinal study with elementary school students in Shanghai that shyness positively predicted increase in maternal and paternal harsh parenting (e.g., "I yell or shout when our child misbehaves," "I use physical punishment as a way of disciplining our child") over time. Similar results have been reported in other studies (e.g., Bullock et al., 2022; Xiao et al., 2021) indicating relations between child shyness and low parental warmth and high parental rejection in urban regions of China today.

Increasingly negative peer attitudes toward shyness along with the social and cultural changes have also been documented in a number of studies conducted in urban China. Chen et al. (2005) conducted a study with elementary school children in Shanghai at different historical times (1990, 1998, and 2002), and found that shyness was positively associated with peer acceptance in the 1990 cohort but with peer rejection in the 2002 cohort. Shyness was associated with both peer acceptance and peer rejection in the 1998 cohort, indicating that peers held ambivalent attitudes toward shy children during this transitional period due to the mixture of new values of social initiative and traditional Chinese values of behavioral restraint and wariness. Bullock et al. (2022) examined one-year longitudinal relations between shyness and peer difficulties in a sample of children in Shanghai during the period of 2013 to 2016 and found that shyness predicted later peer rejection and victimization ("Get picked on or teased by other kids," "Get left out on purpose during activity or play time").

Research on social attitudes toward children's shyness has been mostly conducted in urban regions of China. Traditional values have been maintained to a greater extent in rural than urban regions (Cai et al., 2020). Chen et al. (2011) conducted a study of shyness and social attitudes in a sample of elementary school children in rural China. Shyness was positively associated with peer approval and acceptance, which was similar to what was found in urban Chinese children in the early 1990s. It will be interesting to examine whether shyness becomes more associated with negative adults' and peers' attitudes in rural regions with increasing urbanization in China.

To what extent will traditional Chinese values continue to affect social attitudes as China becomes more urbanized and modernized? The data in Zhang and Xu (2019) study were collected in Shanghai and Hawai'i in 2014. The significant differences found in the samples showed that, when asked about their attitudes about shy classmates, Chinese children were still more willing to play with and be a friend with them than US children were. As Kagitcibasi (2012) and Chen (2015) have contended, it is possible that the ongoing social changes in most countries in the world – due to domestic and transnational migration of populations, advances in information technology and communication, and interactions among political, economic, and cultural systems across regions – have led to integration of diverse values and lifestyles. This pluralist-constructivist perspective suggests that while new values, such as individuality and autonomy, have a significant impact on individual attitudes and behaviors, they may not necessarily replace traditional values, but instead may be integrated into the cultural systems in the society. As such, it may be reasonable to expect that, although shy children experience more negative social evaluations and responses with social changes, adult and peer attitudes in China may not become the same as in Western societies. The relatively greater dispositional tendency of Chinese children to display shy reactions in challenging situations (Chen, 2018) may require the provision of a supportive environment for shy children to maintain a healthy society from a macro-level person-environment goodness of fit perspective. How parents and peers provide support for shy Chinese children to regulate their internal anxiety and fear in social interaction and to express anxiety and fear in a constructive manner should be explored in future research as social changes in China continue to grow in magnitude and intensity.

6.3.2 Shyness and Adjustment

In societies where shyness is regarded as undesirable and abnormal, social attitudes and treatments that shy children receive are likely to make them feel frustrated, concerned, and insecure, especially when it is difficult for them to change their behavior. The unsupportive social experiences and negative reactions of shy children may lead to maladaptive development. In Western countries (e.g., Coplan et al., 2013; Rubin et al., 2009), shyness in childhood and adolescence is associated with adjustment problems in social, school, and psychological areas, including low social status, academic difficulties, negative self-regard, loneliness, and depression. Shy children are more likely than others to display problems in social relationships when they start elementary school (e.g., Coplan et al., 2004). When they realize their social difficulties, shy children may develop negative self-regard and psychological disturbances (e.g., Coplan et al., 2004; Prior et al., 2000; Rubin et al., 1995). Longitudinal studies indicate that shy children, particularly boys, in Western countries, such as Germany and the United States, develop more problems than others in life adjustment, such as delayed entry into marriage, career instability, low occupational status, poor social relationships, and emotional distress in adulthood (Asendorpf et al., 2008; Caspi et al., 1988).

Shyness is associated with fewer adjustment problems in societies where social initiative and self-expression are less valued and encouraged (Chen, 2018). In studies conducted in the 1990s, Chen and colleagues (e.g., Chen et al., 1995; Chen, Dong, & Zhou, 1997) found that shyness in Chinese children was positively associated with leadership status, peer-assessed and teacher-rated competence, academic achievement, and perceived self-worth and negatively associated with learning problems, loneliness, and depression. The results suggest that shy Chinese children were generally well adjusted in various areas. Chen et al. (1999) examined longitudinal relations between childhood shyness and adjustment outcomes in adolescence in Shanghai. Data on shyness were collected from peer assessments in the first wave from a sample of children at eight and ten years of age. A follow-up study was conducted four years later when the children were in the junior high school, with data collected from multiple sources, including teacher ratings, peer evaluations, self-reports, and school records. Shyness in childhood was not associated with adjustment problems in adolescence. Moreover, shyness was positively associated with later teacher-rated competence, leadership, distinguished student-ship, and academic achievement. Shyness was also positively associated with self-perceptions of behavioral competence (e.g., "I usually do the right thing," "I behave myself very well"), although not general self-worth (e.g., "I am happy with myself as a person"). These results suggested that shy children in China continued to perform well, particularly in social and school areas, in the later years.

The studies reporting positive adjustment outcomes of shyness in Chinese children (e.g., Chen et al., 1999) were conducted in the early 1990s. With the massive social and cultural transformations and associated changes in adult and peer attitudes toward shy behavior, it is unsurprising that shy children, particularly in urban regions of China, experience increased adjustment problems today. Chen et al. (2005) found that, unlike their counterparts in a 1992 cohort, shy children in a 2002 cohort no longer had advantages over others in obtaining leadership status and academic achievement in school. Moreover, relative to nonshy children, shy children were rated by teachers as less competent in school performance and reported a higher level of depression. Research conducted since (e.g., An & Eggum-Wilkens, 2019; Liu et al., 2018) has shown that relations between shyness and adjustment problems in Chinese children are similar to those in the 2002 cohort in Chen et al.'s study (2005). Liu, Chen, et al. (2015), for example, found that shyness was negatively associated with teacher-rated school competence, academic achievement, and self-perceptions of general self-worth, and positively associated with loneliness and depression among children and adolescents in urban China. Xiao et al. (2021) found in a sample of elementary and middle school students in Shanghai that self-reported shyness was positively associated with internalizing problems as indexed by teacher-rated internalizing problems and self-reported loneliness and depression.

Consistent with the findings about the positive peer attitudes toward shyness, Chen et al.'s study (2011) showed that shyness was associated with indexes of positive adjustment, such as teacher-rated school competence, leadership status, and academic achievement, in a rural region of China. Thus, shy rural children were likely to achieve social and academic success, whereas their urban counterparts experienced adjustment difficulties. The relations between shyness and adjustment in contemporary rural children may be more similar to those found in urban children as social changes are occurring in most rural regions, although not to the same extent as in urban regions.

Developmental issues should be considered in the study of shyness and adjustment. Liu et al. (2017) examined shyness of children (grades 3 and 4) and adolescents (grades 7 and 8) in a suburban region of a metropolitan center in China, which was characterized by mixed values and lifestyles. Shyness was negatively associated with peer preference in adolescents but not in children. Moreover, shyness was positively associated with feelings of loneliness and depression only in adolescents. According to Liu et al. (2017), the development of social-cognitive abilities may make adolescents more sensitive to new values, such as those of self-direction and assertiveness. At the same time, as adult influence becomes weaker, adolescents may be more likely to make their own judgments, which may undermine the role of the traditional values of group orientation and self-constraint in protecting shy children from developing social and psychological problems.

There are also gender differences in relations between shyness and adjustment. In Western cultures, shyness is perceived as less acceptable in boys than in girls because boys are expected to display more assertive and autonomous behaviors in social interactions (Doey et al., 2014). Shy behavior is also less encouraged in boys than in girls in Chinese society due to the gender-related stereotypical beliefs (Chen, 2019). Men have traditionally been expected to assume greater responsibility than women to maintain and enhance the status and reputation of the family. To successfully fulfill their roles, whereas girls are typically encouraged to help parents with household chores, boys are more encouraged to go out and interact with others and thus experience greater pressure to control their shy behavior. Consistent with the Western literature (Doey et al., 2014; Rubin et al., 2009), research in China has indicated that boys tend to display lower levels of shyness than girls (e.g., Chen et al., 2005; Ding et al., 2020; Liu, Chen, et al., 2015; Yang et al., 2015), although no significant gender differences are found in temperament reactivity or behavioral inhibition in the early years (Chen et al., 1998, 2014). Whereas shyness is often related to more negative, or less positive, adjustment outcomes in boys than in girls in Western countries (Doey et al., 2014; Rubin et al., 2009), no consistent gender differences in the relations have been found in Chinese children (e.g., Chen et al., 2005; Ding et al., 2020; Yang et al., 2015), suggesting that shy boys may not experience more adjustment problems than shy girls. It is unclear what factors serve to hinder the potential inclination of shy boys to develop adjustment problems in China.

In sum, as China changes toward a competitive market-oriented society, particularly in urban regions, shyness has become an increasingly maladaptive behavioral characteristic that is associated with, and predictive of, difficulties in social and psychological adjustment. The negative effects of shyness on adjustment are more evident in adolescence than in childhood. With the social change, researchers and professionals need to explore resources in the family, school, and society and specific strategies that may help shy children cope with challenges and protect them from developing problems. In Chen and Tse's study (2008), although Chinese Canadian children, particularly girls, displayed a higher level of shyness than European Canadian children, shyness was associated with peer victimization and rejection among European Canadian children, but not among Chinese Canadian children. The authors argued that the experience of Chinese Canadian children in the family might help them develop relatively advanced regulatory skills in the early years (e.g., Chen et al., 2003). These skills, in turn, help the children express their internal anxiety in prosocial or other socially acceptable manners when they interact with peers in school. Further research is needed to understand how socialization practices based on integrated diverse cultural beliefs and values affect the development of shy Chinese children.

6.3.3 Regulated Shyness, Unsociability, Social Avoidance, and Related Issues

Xu et al. (2007) argued that, in addition to anxious shyness that has been extensively discussed and studied in Western countries, Chinese children may display another type of shyness – regulated shyness. Regulated shyness is concerned with acquiescent, nonassertive, and unassuming behaviors, such as "behaving modestly" and "not showing-off," in social interactions. Because regulated shy children tend to constrain their behaviors and activities to fit in the group, they are often perceived as well behaved and polite. Xu and colleagues (Xu et al., 2007; Xu & Krieg, 2014) have demonstrated that regulated shyness is positively associated with peer approval and acceptance and prosocial behavior, and negatively associated with loneliness and other internalizing problems.

An important question is to what extent regulated shyness reflects a shy or regulated behavior, if it is not derived from internal anxiety and fear in challenging social situations. The adjustment outcomes of regulated shyness are largely similar to those of regulated behavior or self-control, which is also highly valued in Chinese culture (Zhou et al., 2009). If this is the case, Xu et al.'s work (2007) may be mostly about comparisons between shyness (or anxious shyness) and regulation (or a specific type of regulation such as "not showing-off"), rather than between different types of shyness.

As a major type of social withdrawal, unsociability has received increased attention from researchers (e.g., Chen et al., 2011; Coplan et al., 2019; Liu, Chen, et al., 2015). At the theoretical level, different perspectives have been provided in the Western literature (e.g., Rubin et al., 2009) on the functions of children's unsociability. It is believed that unsociability may lead to a lack of opportunities to learn social and problem-solving skills from others and obtain social support in coping with adjustment difficulties (e.g., Rubin et al., 2015). However, Bowker and Raja (2011) theorized that unsociable children may obtain just enough social experiences for learning and practicing relevant skills because they do not actively avoid social interactions that are initiated by others. Moreover, unsociability or preference for solitude may be viewed as an autonomous expression of personal choice, rather than as an indication of social failure or incompetence (Chen, 2019; Coplan & Armer, 2007). From this perspective, unsociability may be a type of social withdrawal that is not necessarily a risk factor in social and cognitive development. Unsociability in early childhood, indexed mainly by solitary behavior (i.e., quiet exploration and solitary constructive activities) in social settings, is regarded as relatively benign (Coplan et al., 2018; Rubin et al., 2009). In adolescence, the ability and willingness to engage in solitary activities or spend time alone for self-reflection, self-exploration, or stress reduction are also believed to have benefits for well-being (e.g., Larson, 1997; Coplan et al., 2019).

Research findings based on Western children are often mixed – some indicate that unsociable children are viewed as less liked than other children by peers (e.g., Coplan et al., 2019), whereas others indicate that unsociable children do not differ from, or even perform better than, other children on social and school tasks (e.g., Harrist et al., 1997). In general, the literature suggests that unsociability is associated with fewer problems than shyness (Coplan et al., 2019). For example, unsociable children do not appear to be more vulnerable than other children to internalizing problems, such as depressive symptoms, loneliness, and social anxiety (e.g., Coplan, et al., 2013). Cultural values of autonomy and self-decision in Western societies may help reduce negative social evaluations of unsociable behavior, which in turn helps children who display the behavior develop reduced adjustment difficulties.

In Chinese society that emphasizes social connectedness and group affiliation, unsociability or preference for solitude conflicts with the socialization goals. As unsociable children display a lack of intention to interact with, and perhaps attempt to maintain distance from, others, they are likely to be perceived as selfish and anti-collective (Chen et al., 2011), which in turn may impede their adaptive development. This argument has been supported by studies in China, indicating that unsociability is associated with problems in peer relationships and school performance in children and adolescents (e.g., Coplan et al., 2016; Liu, Chen, et al., 2015). For example, unsociable children are more likely than others to be excluded and victimized by peers, have more learning problems, and report higher levels of loneliness and depression (e.g., Coplan et al., 2016; Zhang & Eggum-Wilkens, 2018). Liu, Chen, et al. (2015) found that unsociability (e.g., "Rather plays alone than with others," "Not interested in participating in activities with others") was negatively associated with peer preference and positively associated with loneliness in samples of elementary and middle school students in urban China and Canada, but the associations were significantly stronger in Chinese students than in Canadian students. Moreover, unsociability was negatively associated with academic achievement and perceived self-worth in the Chinese sample, but not in the Canadian sample. In short, unsociable children in China experience more extensive difficulties than their counterparts in Western countries. Moreover, while the macro-level social changes in China have made shyness less adaptive, there is no evidence that they have significantly affected the functional meaning of unsociability. Whether unsociable children become better adjusted as China continues to change toward a more urbanized society in the future merits investigation.

Finally, Ding and colleagues (Ding et al., 2022; Sang et al., 2018) developed a self-report measure of social avoidance in Chinese children and adolescents (e.g., "I actively avoid playing with other children," "I often turn down social invitations from other children because I want to be alone") and assessed its relations with social and psychological adjustment outcomes. The results appeared straightforward – social avoidance was associated with peer rejection and psychological problems, which was similar to what has been reported in Western and other countries (e.g., Bowker & Raja, 2011; Coplan et al., 2013). Some issues concerning children's social avoidance remain to be clarified at theoretical and empirical levels. For example, it is unclear why children actively avoid social interaction. Social avoidance may be an extreme form of shyness, a manifestation of depression or social anxiety, or an indication of general socioemotional maladjustment (Sang et al., 2018). Sang et al. (2018) reported that the mean score of social avoidance was 1.34 ($SD = 0.64$) on a 1 (not at all) to 5 (always) point scale, suggesting that the level of social avoidance was extremely low in Chinese children and adolescents. Whether social avoidance is related to uncommon adverse, perhaps traumatic, experiences or psychopathological functioning needs to be explored. Ding et al. (2022) and Sang et al. (2018) found that social avoidance was correlated with unsociability more strongly than with shyness. Thus, social avoidance may involve social disinterest to a greater extent than social anxiety or fear, which is not consistent with the speculation (Bowker & Raja, 2011; Sang et al., 2018). Further work is needed on social avoidance in Chinese children.

7 Future Directions of Research on Socialization and Socioemotional Development in Chinese Children

Since the early 1990s, research on socialization and socioemotional development in Chinese children has burgeoned. Some of the major findings are described in this Element. This section discusses some future directions for research in this area.

First, China is a large country with fifty-six recognized ethnic groups, each with unique social and cultural features. However, research on socialization and socioemotional development has been conducted almost completely with the Han group. Accordingly, the Element focuses on Han families and children. To avoid ethnocentric and biased views of families and children in the ethnic minority groups, generalization of the findings from Han Chinese needs to be made with caution. More importantly, researchers could profitably explore socialization and development among children of different ethnicities in China. In a study of parental socialization goals, Zhang and Ng (2022) asked adolescents in a northwestern region of China to list the five most important goals that their parents have for them. The sample consisted of two Muslim groups, the Hui and Kazakhs, in addition to Han. Significant differences were found among the groups. Relative to Han parents, parents in the two Muslim groups, particularly Kazakh, were reported to emphasize social relationships more, especially outside the family (e.g., "Make more friends"), proper moral demeanor (e.g., "Have good moral qualities"), and contributions to the society ("Save many lives as a doctor"). In contrast, Han parents were more likely than the Muslim parents to emphasize self-maximization, such as autonomy (e.g., "Make own decisions"), and psychological well-being (e.g., "Be happy"). According to Zhang and Ng (2022), Han parents are more exposed to individualistic values and thus are more ready to endorse individuality, self-expression, and pursuing personal happiness as socialization goals. In contrast, tribal identity continues to be emphasized in daily activities of Kazakhs, and tribal members are encouraged to support one another with pooled resources. Consequently, orientation to the collective that extends beyond the family is a main feature of the socialization belief system of Kazakh parents. Although Zhang and Ng (2022)'s study relied on adolescent reports, the results may help us understand similarities and differences in parental

socialization goals between the Muslim and Han families. Research on socialization and socioemotional development in ethnic minority groups in China will
provide rich opportunities to understand the role of contextual factors in human
development.

Second, although the cultural background of the Chinese society is relatively
homogenous with Confucianism exerting a profound impact on social interactions and individual behaviors, substantial differences exist across regions
within China, which need to be considered in the study of human development.
For example, it was reported that people in rice-growing southern China were
more interdependent and holistic-thinking than people in the wheat-growing
north (Talhelm et al., 2014). It would be interesting to investigate South–North
differences in China on socialization values and practices and socioemotional
development. In addition, dramatic social changes have been occurring in both
urban and rural regions of China, leading to coexistence of new Western and
traditional Chinese values and lifestyles. Consequently, the exposure to different values and lifestyles has become a common experience of children. Thus,
parent–child and peer interactions and the adjustment of children with different
socioemotional characteristics should be understood in the culturally diverse
environment.

Third, many studies of socialization and socioemotional development in
Chinese children have been conducted using a cross-cultural approach, typically
in explicit or implicit comparison with samples of children in North America and
Western Europe. The results are often interpreted in terms of collectivistic versus
individualistic cultural values as they are well represented by Chinese and Western
societies, respectively (Chen & French, 2008; Oyserman et al., 2002). Despite
concerns and criticisms about the oversimplicity of broad cultural categories,
research using this approach has provided useful information on similarities and
differences between Chinese and Western children on socialization experiences
and developmental patterns. Nevertheless, the theoretical framework of collectivism versus individualism has been recognized for its inadequacy in describing
complex cultural systems. Researchers should pay greater attention to the influence of specific cultural beliefs and values, such as filial piety and strengthening in
adversity, on socialization and child development in China.

Fourth, research with Chinese children, with or without comparison with
a non-Chinese sample, has mostly relied on the Western theories (e.g.,
Baumrind's parenting styles, the Asendorpf's model of social withdrawal) and
methods (e.g., Achenbach's Child Behavior Checklist). The adoption of existing theories and methods may be a necessary step in the study of Chinese
children. However, researchers should be aware of the limitations of the theories
and methods given that they were developed according to social and cultural

circumstances in Western societies. As Chao (1994) argued, for example, power-assertive parenting based on parental care and concern may not fit with either the authoritarian or authoritative style in Baumrind's theory. Chao (1994) explored the indigenous Chinese or Asian parenting style by proposing the concept of *guan*. To expand this and related ideas (Cheah et al., 2019; Chen, Fu, et al., 2019; Ho, 1986; Tobin et al., 1989), this Element discusses CBPAP of Chinese parents in terms of its affective and behavioral manifestations in parent–child interactions, functions in serving the group-oriented socialization goals, and potential influence on child development in specific domains. How Chinese parents use power assertion in the context of care or express care in power-assertive behavior (e.g., expressing concerns when children fall behind social expectations, emphasizing responsibility for the family in childrearing, encouraging children to appreciate parental sacrifices for them to achieve success) and how CBPAP contributes to social, school, and psychological adjustment in Chinese children merit exploration.

Finally, the review and discussion of socioemotional development in this Element focus mainly on two fundamental dimensions of early socioemotional functioning, temperamental reactivity and self-control, as well as associated social behaviors in childhood and adolescence. Researchers have investigated other characteristics and behaviors in Chinese children, such as emotional expressivity (Camras et al., 1998; Wang, 2008), modesty (Ma et al., 2019), and self-compassion (Yang et al., 2021). It will be crucial to build on these research initiatives and engage in continuous explorations to achieve a more comprehensive and in-depth understanding of socioemotional development in Chinese children.

8 Conclusions

Chinese children display distinct socioemotional characteristics in the early years of life. Compared with their Western counterparts, Chinese children are more reactive to challenging and stressful situations, as indicated by their inhibited and vigilant behaviors in interactions with strangers and in other novel settings. Chinese children also display a higher level of self-control than Western children, as shown in their persistence on task completion, suppression of impulsive behavior to achieve desired goals, and compliance with adults' directions and social standards. The early characteristics constitute a dispositional foundation for the development of major social behaviors, such as prosocial behavior, aggression, and shyness. At the same time, Chinese culture plays a significant role in shaping socialization conditions, particularly childrearing goals and practices, as well as adults' and peers' attitudes and responses toward specific behaviors that children display in social interactions. The culturally directed socialization processes determine, in part, the developmental patterns of socioemotional functioning.

As China is changing toward a competitive, market-oriented society, particularly in urban regions, socioemotional characteristics and behaviors that have traditionally been valued, such as obedience and shyness, become increasingly maladaptive and associated with adjustment problems. At the same time, characteristics and behaviors that have traditionally been neglected, such as initiative-taking, active exploration, and self-direction, are required to obtain success in the competitive environment and thus gradually appreciated and encouraged in socialization. The social change may also promote integration of traditional and new values (e.g., those about autonomy and connectedness), which serve different functions in human development for pursuing personal goals and maintaining social support systems. Socialization experiences in the context of diverse cultural beliefs and values may help children develop sophisticated competencies and qualities that allow them to function flexibly and effectively in different circumstances.

Research on socialization and socioemotional development in Chinese children should continue to explore distinct developmental patterns and processes, especially in ethnic groups beyond Han Chinese and in regions with different backgrounds. It will be important to investigate relevant issues in human development in Chinese society using culturally appropriate theoretical frameworks and scientifically rigorous methods. In addition, researchers should work with parents, educators, policymakers, and professionals to develop effective programs and strategies based on research findings to help enhance socioemotional well-being of Chinese children.

References

Ahadi, S. A., Rothbart, M. K., & Ye, R. (1993). Children's temperament in the US and China: Similarities and differences. *European Journal of Personality*, 7(5), 359–377. https://doi.org/10.1002/per.2410070506.

An, D., & Eggum-Wilkens, N. D. (2019). Do cultural orientations moderate the relation between Chinese adolescents' shyness and depressive symptoms? It depends on their academic achievement. *Social Development*, 28(4), 908–926. https://doi.org/10.1111/sode.12365.

Asendorpf, J. B. (1990). Beyond social withdrawal: Shyness, unsociability, and peer avoidance. *Human Development*, 33(4–5), 250–259. https://doi.org/10.1159/000276522.

Asendorpf, J. B. (1991). Development of inhibited children's coping with unfamiliarity. *Child Development*, 62(6), 1460–1474. https://doi.org/10.2307/1130819.

Asendorpf, J. B., Denissen, J. J. A., & van Aken, M. A. G. (2008). Inhibited and aggressive preschool children at 23 years of age: Personality and social transition into adulthood. *Developmental Psychology*, 44(4), 997–1011. https://doi.org/10.1037/0012-1649.44.4.997.

Bandura, A. (1977). *Social learning theory*. Hoboken, New Jersey: Prentice-Hall.

Baumrind, D. (1971). Current patterns of parental authority. *Developmental Psychology*, 4(1, Pt.2), 1–103. https://doi.org/10.1037/h0030372.

Bergeron, N., & Schneider, B. H. (2005). Explaining cross-national differences in peer-directed aggression: A quantitative synthesis. *Aggressive Behavior*, 31(2), 116–137. https://doi.org/10.1002/ab.20049.

Bonanno, G. A. (2004). Loss, trauma, and human resilience: Have we underestimated the human capacity to thrive after extremely aversive events? *American Psychologist*, 59(1), 20–28. https://doi.org/10.1037/0003-066X.59.1.20.

Bond, M. H. (2004). Culture and aggression: From context to coercion. *Personality and Social Psychology Review*, 8(1), 62–78. https://doi.org/10.1207/s15327957pspr0801_3.

Bornstein, M. H. (1995). Form and function: Implications for studies of culture and human development. *Culture and Psychology*, 1, 123–137. https://doi.org/10.1177/1354067X9511009.

Bornstein, M. H., & Esposito, G. (2020). Cross-cultural perspectives on parent–infant interactions. In J. J. Lockman & C. S. Tamis-LeMonda

(Eds.), *The Cambridge handbook of infant development: Brain, behavior, and cultural context* (pp. 805–831). Cambridge, UK: Cambridge University Press. https://doi.org/10.1017/9781108351959.029.

Bornstein, M. H., & Lansford, J. E. (2019). Culture and family functioning. In B. H. Fiese, M. Celano, K. Deater-Deckard, E. N. Jouriles, & M. A. Whisman (Eds.), *APA handbook of contemporary family psychology: Applications and broad impact of family psychology* (pp. 417–436). Washington, DC: American Psychological Association. https://doi.org/10.1037/0000100-026.

Bowker, J. C., & Raja, R. (2011). Social withdrawal subtypes during early adolescence in India. *Journal of Abnormal Child Psychology, 39*(2), 201–212. https://doi.org/10.1007/s10802-010-9461-7.

Bowlby, J. (1969). *Attachment and loss: Vol. I. Attachment.* New York: Basic Books.

Bullock, A., Xiao, B., Liu, J., Coplan, R. J., & Chen, X. (2022). Shyness, parent–child relationships, and peer difficulties during the middle school transition. *Journal of Child and Family Studies, 31*(1), 86–98. https://doi.org/10.1007/s10826-021-01979-3.

Cai, H., Huang, Z., Lin, L. et al. (2020). The psychological change of the Chinese people over the past half century: A literature review. *Advances in Psychological Science, 28*(10), 1599–1688. https://doi.org/10.3724/SP.J.1042.2020.01599.

Cambridge Chinese Classics (2022). *The Three-Character Classic.* www.camcc.org/reading-group/adhoc/08022014#text.

Camras, L., Kolmodin, K., & Chen, Y. (2008). Mothers' self-reported emotional expression in Mainland Chinese, Chinese American and European American families. *International Journal of Behavioral Development, 32*(5), 459–463. https://doi.org/10.1177/0165025408093665.

Camras, L. A., Oster, H., Campos, J. et al. (1998). Production of emotional facial expressions in European American, Japanese, and Chinese infants. *Developmental Psychology, 34*(4), 616–628. https://doi.org/10.1037/0012-1649.34.4.616.

Caspi, A., Elder, G. H., & Bem, D. J. (1988). Moving away from the world: Life-course patterns of shy children. *Developmental Psychology, 24*(6), 824–831. https://doi.org/10.1037/0012-1649.24.6.824.

Chao, R. K. (1994). Beyond parental control and authoritarian parenting style: Understanding Chinese parenting through the cultural notion of training. *Child Development, 65*(4), 1111–1119. https://doi.org/10.2307/1131308.

Chao, R. K. (1995). Chinese and European American cultural models of the self reflected in mothers' childrearing beliefs. *Ethos, 23*(3), 328–354. https://doi.org/10.1525/eth.1995.23.3.02a00030.

Chao, R. K., & Aque, C. (2009). Interpretations of parental control by Asian immigrant and European American youth. *Journal of Family Psychology*, *23*(3), 342–354. https://doi.org/10.1037/a0015828.

Cheah, C. S. L., & Li, J. (2010). Parenting of young immigrant Chinese children: Challenges facing their social emotional and intellectual development. In E. L. Grigorenko & R. Takanishi (Eds.), *Immigration, diversity, and education* (pp. 225–241). New York: Routledge.

Cheah, C. S. L., Li, J., Zhou, N., Yamamoto, Y., & Leung, C. Y. (2015). Understanding Chinese immigrant and European American mothers' expressions of warmth. *Developmental Psychology*, *51*(12), 1802–1811. https://doi.org/10.1037/a0039855.

Cheah, C. S. L., Yu, J., Liu, J., & Coplan, R. J. (2019). Children's cognitive appraisal moderates associations between psychologically controlling parenting and children's depressive symptoms. *Journal of Adolescence*, *76*, 109–119. https://doi.org/10.1016/j.adolescence.2019.08.005.

Chen, C., Greenberger, E., Lester, J., Dong, Q., & Guo, M.-S. (1998). A cross-cultural study of family and peer correlates of adolescent misconduct. *Developmental Psychology*, *34*(4), 770–781. https://doi.org/10.1037/0012-1649.34.4.770.

Chen, L., Chen, X., Zhao, Z. et al. (2019). Predicting substance use and deviant behavior from prosociality and sociability in adolescents. *Journal of Youth and Adolescence*, *48*(4), 744–752. https://doi.org/10.1007/s10964-018-0940-4.

Chen, X. (2010). Socioemotional development in Chinese children. In M. H. Bond (Ed.), *Handbook of Chinese psychology* (pp. 37–52). Oxford: Oxford University Press.

Chen, X. (2012). Culture, peer interaction, and socioemotional development. *Child Development Perspectives*, *6*(1), 27–34. https://doi.org/10.1111/j.1750-8606.2011.00187.x.

Chen, X. (2015). Exploring the implications of social change for human development: Perspectives, issues, and future directions. *International Journal of Psychology*, *50*(1), 56–59. https://doi.org/10.1002/ijop.12128.

Chen, X. (2018). Culture, temperament, and social and psychological adjustment. *Developmental Review*, *50*, 42–53. https://doi.org/10.1016/j.dr.2018.03.004.

Chen, X. (2019). Culture and shyness in childhood and adolescence. *New Ideas in Psychology*, *53*, 58–66. https://doi.org/10.1016/j.newideapsych.2018.04.007

Chen, X. (2020). Exploring cultural meanings of adaptive and maladaptive behaviors in children and adolescents: A contextual-developmental perspective. *International Journal of Behavioral Development*, *44*(3), 256–265. https://doi.org/10.1177/0165025419877797.

Chen, X., Bian, Y., Xin, T., Wang, L., & Silbereisen, R. K. (2010). Perceived social change and childrearing attitudes in China. *European Psychologist, 15*(4), 260–270. https://doi.org/10.1027/1016-9040/a000060.

Chen, X., Cen, G., Li, D., & He, Y. (2005). Social functioning and adjustment in Chinese children: The imprint of historical time. *Child Development, 76*(1), 182–195. https://doi.org/10.1111/j.1467-8624.2005.00838.x.

Chen, X., Chang, L., Liu, H., & He, Y. (2008). Effects of the peer group on the development of social functioning and academic achievement: A longitudinal study in Chinese children. *Child Development, 79*(2), 235–251. https://doi.org/10.1111/j.1467-8624.2007.01123.x.

Chen, X., & Chen, H. (2010). Children's socioemotional functioning and adjustment in the changing Chinese society. In R. K. Silbereisen & X. Chen (Eds.), *Social change and human development: Concepts and results* (pp. 209–226). London: Sage.

Chen, X., Chen, H., Li, D., & Wang, L. (2009). Early childhood behavioral inhibition and social and school adjustment in Chinese children: A 5-year longitudinal study. *Child Development, 80*(6), 1692–1704. https://doi.org/10.1111/j.1467-8624.2009.01362.x.

Chen, X., Chen, X., Zhao, S. et al. (2021). Autonomy- and connectedness-oriented behaviors of toddlers and mothers at different historical times in urban China. *Developmental Psychology, 57*(8), 1254–1260. https://doi.org/10.1037/dev0001224.

Chen, X., DeSouza, A. T., Chen, H., & Wang, L. (2006). Reticent behavior and experiences in peer interactions in Chinese and Canadian children. *Developmental Psychology, 42*(4), 656–665. https://doi.org/10.1037/0012-1649.42.4.656.

Chen, X., Dong, Q., & Zhou, H. (1997). Authoritative and authoritarian parenting practices and social and school performance in Chinese children. *International Journal of Behavioral Development, 21*(4), 855–873. https://doi.org/10.1080/016502597384703.

Chen, X., & French, D. C. (2008). Children's social competence in cultural context. *Annual Review of Psychology, 59*, 591–616. https://doi.org/10.1146/annurev.psych.59.103006.093606.

Chen, X., Fu, R., Li, D. et al. (2021). Behavioral inhibition in early childhood and adjustment in late adolescence in China. *Child Development, 92*(3), 994–1010. https://doi.org/10.1111/cdev.13463.

Chen, X., Fu, R., Liu, J. et al. (2018). Social sensitivity and social, school, and psychological adjustment among children across contexts. *Developmental Psychology, 54*(6), 1124–1134. https://doi.org/10.1037/dev0000496.

Chen, X., Fu, R., & Yiu, W. Y. V. (2019). Culture and parenting. In M. H. Bornstein (Ed.), *Handbook of parenting: Biology and ecology of parenting* (pp. 448–473). New York: Routledge. https://doi.org/10.4324/9780429401459-14.

Chen, X., Hastings, P. D., Rubin, K. H. et al. (1998). Child-rearing attitudes and behavioral inhibition in Chinese and Canadian toddlers: A cross-cultural study. *Developmental Psychology, 34*(4), 677–686. https://doi.org/10.1037/0012-1649.34.4.677.

Chen, X., He, Y., De Oliveira, A. M. et al. (2004). Loneliness and social adaptation in Brazilian, Canadian, Chinese and Italian children. *Journal of Child Psychology and Psychiatry, 45*(8), 1373–1384. https://doi.org/10.1111/j.1469-7610.2004.00329.x.

Chen, X., Kaspar, V., Zhang, Y., Wang. L., & Zheng, S. (2004). Peer relationships among Chinese and North American boys: A cross-cultural perspective. In N. Way & J. Chu (Eds.), *Adolescent boys in context* (pp. 197–218). New York: New York University Press.

Chen, X., Lee, J., & Chen, L. (2018). Culture and peer relationships. In W. M. Bukowski, B. Laursen, & K. H. Rubin (Eds.), *Handbook of peer interactions, relationships, and groups* (pp. 552–570). New York: Guilford.

Chen, X., & Li, D. (2012). Parental encouragement of initiative-taking and adjustment in Chinese children from rural, urban, and urbanized families. *Journal of Family Psychology, 26*(6), 927–936. https://doi.org/10.1037/a0030708.

Chen, X., Li, D., Li, Z., Li, B., & Liu, M. (2000). Sociable and prosocial dimensions of social competence in Chinese children: Common and unique contributions to social, academic and psychological adjustment. *Developmental Psychology, 36*(3), 302–314. https://doi.org/10.1037//0012-1649.36.3.302.

Chen, X., Li, D., Liu, J., Chen, H., & Zhao, S. (2018). Judgments of damage to public versus private property in Chinese children at different historical times. *Developmental Science, 21*(1), e12506. https://doi.org/10.1111/desc.12506.

Chen, X., Li, D., Xu, X. et al. (2019). School adjustment of children from rural migrant families in urban China. *Journal of School Psychology, 72*, 14–28. https://doi.org/10.1016/j.jsp.2018.12.003.

Chen, X., Liu, J., Ellis, W., & Zarbatany, L. (2016). Social sensitivity and adjustment in Chinese and Canadian children. *Child Development, 87*(4), 1115–1129. https://doi.org/10.1111/cdev.12514.

Chen, X., Liu, M., & Li, D. (2000). Parental warmth, control, and indulgence and their relations to adjustment in Chinese children: A longitudinal study. *Journal of Family Psychology, 14*(3), 401–419. https://doi.org/10.1037/0893-3200.14.3.401.

Chen, X., Liu, M., Rubin, K. H. et al. (2002). Sociability and prosocial orientation as predictors of youth adjustment: A seven-year longitudinal study in a Chinese sample. *International Journal of Behavioral Development, 26*(2), 128–136. https://doi.org/10.1080/01650250042000690.

Chen, X., Rubin, K. H., & Li, Z. (1995). Social functioning and adjustment in Chinese children: A longitudinal study. *Developmental Psychology, 31*(4), 531–539. https://doi.org/10.1037/0012-1649.31.4.531.

Chen, X., Rubin, K. H., & Li, B. (1997). Maternal acceptance and social and school adjustment in Chinese children: A four-year longitudinal study. *Merrill-Palmer Quarterly, 43*(4), 663–681.

Chen, X., Rubin, K. H., Li, B., & Li, D. (1999). Adolescent outcomes of social functioning in Chinese children. *International Journal of Behavioral Development, 23*(1), 199–223. https://doi.org/10.1080/016502599384071.

Chen, X., Rubin, K. H., Liu, M. et al. (2003). Compliance in Chinese and Canadian toddlers: A cross-cultural study. *International Journal of Behavioral Development, 27*(5), 428–436. https://doi.org/10.1080/0165025 0344000046.

Chen, X., Rubin, K. H., & Sun, Y. (1992). Social reputation and peer relationships in Chinese and Canadian children: A cross-cultural study. *Child Development, 63*(6), 1336–1343. https://doi.org/10.2307/1131559.

Chen, X., & Schmidt, L. A. (2015). Temperament and personality. In M. E. Lamb & R. M. Lerner (Eds.), *Handbook of child psychology and developmental science: Socioemotional processes* (pp. 152–200). Hoboken, NJ: John Wiley. https://doi.org/10.1002/9781118963418.childpsy305.

Chen, X., & Tse, H. C. (2008). Social functioning and adjustment in Canadian-born children with Chinese and European backgrounds. *Developmental Psychology, 44*(4), 1184–1189. https://doi.org/10.1037/0012-1649.44.4.1184.

Chen, X., Wang, L., & Cao, R. (2011). Shyness-sensitivity and unsociability in rural Chinese children: Relations with social, school, and psychological adjustment. *Child Development, 82*(5), 1531–1543. https://doi.org/10.1111/j.1467-8624.2011.01616.x.

Chen, X., Zhang, G., Chen, H., & Li, D. (2012). Performance on delay tasks in early childhood predicted socioemotional and school adjustment nine years later: A longitudinal study in Chinese children. *International Perspectives in Psychology: Research, Practice, Consultation, 1*(1), 3–14. https://doi.org/10.1037/a0026363.

Chen, X., Zhang, G., Liang, Z. et al. (2014). The association between 5-HTTLPR gene polymorphism and behavioral inhibition in Chinese toddlers. *Developmental Psychobiology, 56*(7), 1601–1608. https://doi.org/10.1002/dev.21253.

Chen, X., Zhou, J., Liu, J., Li, D., & Liu, S. (2022). Academic performance and depression in Chinese children: Same-domain and cross-domain effects in friendships. *Child Development.* https://doi.org/10.1111/cdev.13864.

Cheung, R. Y. M., & Park, I. J. K. (2010). Anger suppression, interdependent self-construal, and depression among Asian American and European American college students. *Cultural Diversity and Ethnic Minority Psychology, 16*(4), 517–525. https://doi.org/10.1037/a0020655.

Chiao, J. Y., & Blizinsky, K. D. (2010). Culture-gene coevolution of individualism-collectivism and the serotonin transporter gene. *Proceedings of the Royal Society B: Biological Sciences, 277*(1681), 529–537. https://doi.org/10.1098/rspb.2009.1650.

Coplan, R. J., & Armer, M. (2007). A "multitude" of solitude: A closer look at social withdrawal and nonsocial play in early childhood. *Child Development Perspectives, 1*(1), 26–32. https://doi.org/10.1111/j.1750-8606.2007.00006.x.

Coplan, R. J., Liu, J., Ooi, L. L. et al. (2016). A person-oriented analysis of social withdrawal in Chinese children. *Social Development, 25*(4), 794–811. https://doi.org/10.1111/sode.12181.

Coplan, R. J., Ooi, L. L., & Baldwin, D. (2019). Does it matter when we want to be alone? Exploring developmental timing effects in the implications of unsociability. *New Ideas in Psychology, 53*, 47–57. https://doi.org/10.1016/j.newideapsych.2018.01.001.

Coplan, R. J., Ooi, B., Xiao, B., & Rose-Krasnor, L. (2018). Assessment and implications of social withdrawal in early childhood: A first look at social avoidance. *Social Development, 27*(1), 125–139. https://doi.org/10.1111/sode.12258.

Coplan, R. J., Prakash, K., O'Neil, K., & Armer, M. (2004). Do you "want" to play? Distinguishing between conflicted shyness and social disinterest in early childhood. *Developmental Psychology, 40*(2), 244–258. https://doi.org/10.1037/0012-1649.40.2.244.

Coplan, R. J., Rose-Krasnor, L., Weeks, M. et al. (2013). Alone is a crowd: Social motivations, social withdrawal, and socioemotional functioning in later childhood. *Developmental Psychology, 49*(5), 861–875. https://doi.org/10.1037/a0028861.

Crick, N. R., & Grotpeter, J. K. (1995). Relational aggression, gender, and social-psychological adjustment. *Child Development, 66*(3), 710–722. https://doi.org/10.2307/1131945.

Crystal, D. S., Chen, C., Fuligni, A. J. et al. (1994). Psychological maladjustment and academic achievement: A cross-cultural study of Japanese, Chinese, and American high school students. *Child Development*, *65*(3), 738–753. https://doi.org/10.2307/1131415.

Ding, N., Frohnwieser, A., Miller, R., & Clayton, N. S. (2021). Waiting for the better reward: Comparison of delay of gratification in young children across two cultures. *PLoS ONE*, 16(9), e0256966. https://doi.org/10.1371/journal.pone.0256966.

Ding, Q., Li, D., Zhou, Y., Dong, H., & Luo, J. (2017). Perceived parental monitoring and adolescent internet addiction: A moderated mediation model. *Addictive Behavior*, *74*, 48–54. https://doi.org/10.1016/j.addbeh.2017.05.033.

Ding, X., Chen, X., Fu, R., Li, D., & Liu, J. (2020). Relations of shyness and unsociability with adjustment in migrant and non-migrant children in urban China. *Journal of Abnormal Child Psychology*, *48*(2), 289–300. https://doi.org/10.1007/s10802-019-00583-w.

Ding, X., Zhang, W., Ooi, L. L. et al. (2022). Longitudinal relations between social avoidance, academic achievement, and adjustment in Chinese children. *Journal of Applied Developmental Psychology*, *79*, 101385. https://doi.org/10.1016/j.appdev.2021.101385.

Doan, S. N., Tardif, T., Miller, A. et al. (2017). Consequences of "tiger" parenting: A cross-cultural study of maternal psychological control and children's cortisol stress response. *Developmental Science*, *20*(3). https://doi.org/10.1111/desc.12404.

Doey, L., Coplan, R. J., & Kingsbury, M. (2014). Bashful boys and coy girls: A review of gender differences in childhood shyness. *Sex Roles: A Journal of Research*, *70*(7–8), 255–266. https://doi.org/10.1007/s11199-013-0317-9.

Dornbusch, S. M., Ritter, P. L., Leiderman, P. H., Roberts, D. F., & Fraleigh, M. J. (1987). The relation of parenting style to adolescent school performance. *Child Development*, *58*(5), 1244–1257. https://doi.org/10.2307/1130618.

Dweck, C. S. (1999). *Self-theories: Their role in motivation, personality, and development*. Philadelphia, PA: The Psychology Press. https://doi.org/10.4324/9781315783048.

Eisenberg, N., Ma, Y., Chang, L. et al. (2007). Relations of effortful control, reactive undercontrol, and anger to Chinese children's adjustment. *Development and Psychopathology*, *19*(2), 385–409. https://doi.org/10.1017/S0954579407070198.

Eisenberg, N., Spinrad, T. L., & Knafo-Noam, A. (2015). Prosocial development. In M. E. Lamb & R. M. Lerner (Eds.), *Handbook of child psychology and developmental science: Socioemotional processes* (pp. 610–656). Hoboken, NJ: John Wiley. https://doi.org/10.1002/9781118963418.childpsy315.

Eisenberg, N., Zhou, Q., Liew, J., Champion, C., & Pidada, S. U. (2006). Emotion, emotion-related regulation, and social functioning. In X. Chen, D. C. French, & B. H. Schneider (Eds.), *Peer relationships in cultural context* (pp. 170–197). New York, NY: Cambridge University Press.

Eisner, M. P., & Malti, T. (2015). Aggressive and violent behavior. In M. E. Lamb & R. M. Lerner (Eds.), *Handbook of child psychology and developmental science: Socioemotional processes* (pp. 794–841). Hoboken, NJ: John Wiley. https://doi.org/10.1002/9781118963418.childpsy319.

Fox, N. A., Henderson, H. A., Marshall, P. J., Nichols, K. E., & Ghera, M. M. (2005). Behavioral inhibition: Linking biology and behavior within a developmental framework. *Annual Review of Psychology, 56*, 235–262. https://doi.org/10.1146/annurev.psych.55.090902.141532.

French, D. C., Chen, X., Chung, J. et al. (2011). Four children and one toy: Chinese and Canadian children faced with potential conflict over a limited resource. *Child Development, 82*(3), 830–841. https://doi.org/10.1111/j.1467-8624.2011.01581.x.

French, D. C., Pidada, S., & Victor, A. (2005). Friendships of Indonesian and United States youth. *International Journal of Behavioral Development, 29*(4), 304–313. https://doi.org/10.1080/01650250544000080.

Fu, X., Kou, Y., & Yang, Y. (2015). Materialistic values among Chinese adolescents: Effects of parental rejection and self-esteem. *Child Youth Care Forum, 44*(1), 43–57. https://doi.org/10.1007/s10566-014-9269-7.

Fuligni, A. J., Witkow, M., & Garcia, C. (2005). Ethnic identity and the academic adjustment of adolescents from Mexican, Chinese, and European backgrounds. *Developmental Psychology, 41*(5), 799–811. https://doi.org/10.1037/0012-1649.41.5.799.

Fung, H. (2006). Affect and early moral socialization: Some insights and contributions from indigenous psychological studies in Taiwan. In K. Uichol, K. S. Yang, & K. K. Hwang (Eds.), *Indigenous and cultural psychology: Understanding people in context* (pp. 175–196). New York: Springer.

Fung, H. (1999). Becoming a moral child: The socialization of shame among young Chinese children. *Ethos, 27*(2), 180–209. https://doi.org/10.1525/eth.1999.27.2.180.

Fung, J., & Lau, A. S. (2012). Tough love or hostile domination? Psychological control and relational induction in cultural context. *Journal of Family Psychology, 26*(6), 966–975. https://doi.org/10.1037/a0030457.

Furman, W., & Buhrmester, D. (1985). Children's perceptions of the personal relationships in their social networks. *Developmental Psychology, 21*(6), 1016–1024. https://doi.org/10.1037/0012-1649.21.6.1016.

Gao, Y., Zhang, W., & Fung, A. L. (2015). The associations between parenting styles and proactive and reactive aggression in Hong Kong children and adolescents. *International Journal of Psychology, 50*(6), 463–471. https://doi.org/10.1002/ijop.12104.

Garmezy, N. (1971). Vulnerability research and the issue of primary prevention. *American Journal of Orthopsychiatry, 41*(1), 101–116. https://doi.org/10.1111/j.1939-0025.1971.tb01111.x.

Gartstein, M. A., Gonzalez-Salinas, C., Carranza, J. A. et al. (2006). Studying cross-cultural differences in the development of infant temperament: People's Republic of China, the United States of America, and Spain. *Child Psychiatry and Human Development, 37*(2), 145–161. https://doi.org/10.1007/s10578-006-0025-6.

Greenberger, E., Chen, C., Beam, M., Whang, S.-M., & Dong, Q. (2000). The perceived social contexts of adolescents' misconduct: A comparative study of youths in three cultures. *Journal of Research on Adolescence, 10*(3), 365–388. https://doi.org/10.1207/SJRA1003_7.

Greenfield, P. M. (2009). Linking social change and developmental change: Shifting pathways of human development. *Developmental Psychology, 45*(2), 401–418. https://doi.org/10.1037/a0014726.

Greenfield, P. M., Suzuki, L. K., & Rothstein-Fisch, C. (2006). Cultural Pathways through Human Development. In K. A. Renninger, I. E. Sigel, W. Damon, & R. M. Lerner (Eds.), *Handbook of child psychology: Child psychology in practice* (pp. 655–699). Hoboken, NJ: John Wiley.

Hane, A. A., Cheah, C., Rubin, K. H., & Fox, N. A. (2008). The role of maternal behavior in the relation between shyness and social reticence in early childhood and social withdrawal in middle childhood. *Social Development, 17*(4), 795–811. https://doi.org/10.1111/j.1467-9507.2008.00481.x.

Harrist, A. W., Zaia, A. F., Bates, J. E., Dodge, K. A., & Pettit, G. S. (1997). Subtypes of social withdrawal in early childhood: Sociometric status and social-cognitive differences across four years. *Child Development, 68*(2), 278–294. https://doi.org/10.2307/1131850.

Hartup, W. W. (1989). Social relationships and their developmental significance. *American Psychologist, 44*(2), 120–126. https://doi.org/10.1037/0003-066X.44.2.120.

Hartup, W. W. (1996). The company they keep: Friendships and their developmental significance. *Child Development, 67*(1), 1–13. https://doi.org/10.2307/1131681.

Hawley, P. H., & Bower, A. R. (2018). Evolution and peer relations: Considering the functional roles of aggression and prosociality. In W. M. Bukowski, B. Laursen, & K. H. Rubin (Eds.), *Handbook of peer interactions, relationships, and groups* (pp. 106–122). New York : The Guilford Press.

He, Y., Yuan, K., Sun, L., & Bian, Y. (2019). A cross-lagged model of the link between parental psychological control and adolescent aggression. *Journal of Adolescence*, *74*, 103–112. https://doi.org/10.1016/j.adolescence.2019.05.007.

Heine, S. J., Takemoto, T., Moskalenko, S., Lasaleta, J., & Henrich, J. (2008). Mirrors in the head: Cultural variation in objective self-awareness. *Personality and Social Psychology Bulletin*, *34*(7), 879–887. http://doi.org/10.1177/0146167208316921.

Henrich, C. C., Blatt, S. J., Kuperminc, G. P., Zohar, A., & Leadbeater, B. J. (2001). Levels of interpersonal concerns and social functioning in early adolescent boys and girls. *Journal of Personality Assessment*, *76*(1), 48–67. https://doi.org/10.1207/S15327752JPA7601_3.

Heyman, G. D., Fu, G., & Lee, K. (2008). Reasoning about the disclosure of success and failure to friends among children in the United States and China. *Developmental Psychology*, *44*(4), 908–918. https://doi.org/10.1037/0012-1649.44.4.908.

Ho, D. Y. F. (1986). Chinese pattern of socialization: A critical review. In M. H. Bond (Ed.), *The psychology of the Chinese people* (pp. 1–37). New York: Oxford University Press.

Huang, Y., Bullock, A., Liu, J., Wang, Z., Xu, G., Sang, B. (2022). Co-rumination with friends exacerbates association between peer victimization and adjustment in adolescence. *Journal of Applied Developmental Psychology*, *80*, 101410. https://doi.org/10.1016/j.appdev.2022.101410.

Huntsinger, C. S., & Jose, P. E. (2009). Relations among parental acceptance and control and children's social adjustment in Chinese American and European American families. *Journal of Family Psychology*, *23*(3), 321–330. https://doi.org/10.1037/a0015812.

Huntsinger, C. S., & Jose, P. E. (2006). A longitudinal investigation of personality and social adjustment among Chinese American and European American adolescents. *Child Development*, *77*(5), 1309–1324. https://doi.org/10.1111/j.1467-8624.2006.00936.x.

Ip, K. I., Felt, B., Wang, L. et al. (2021). Are preschoolers' neurobiological stress systems responsive to culturally relevant contexts? *Psychological Science*, *32*(7), 998–1010. https://doi.org/10.1177/0956797621994233.

Jessor, R., Turbin, M. S., Costa, F. M. et al. (2003). Adolescent problem behavior in China and the United States: A cross-national study of psychosocial protective factors. *Journal of Research on Adolescence, 13*(3), 329–360. https://doi.org/10.1111/1532-7795.1303004.

Ji, L., Zhang, W., & Jones, K. (2016). Children's experience of and attitudes towards bullying and victimization: A cross-cultural comparison between China and England. In P. K. Smith, K. Kwak, & Y. Toda (Eds.), *School bullying in different cultures: Eastern and Western perspectives* (pp. 170–188). Cambridge, UK: Cambridge University Press. https://doi.org/10.1017/CBO9781139410878.012.

Jin, G., Fu, R., Li, D., Chen, X., & Liu, J. (2021). Longitudinal associations between prosociality and depressive symptoms in Chinese children: The mediating role of peer preference. *Journal of Youth and Adolescence, 51*(5), 956–966. https://doi.org/10.1007/s10964-021-01501-4.

Jose, P. E., Huntsinger, C. S., Huntsinger, P. R., & Liaw, F.-R. (2000). Parental values and practices relevant to young children's social development in Taiwan and the United States. *Journal of Cross-Cultural Psychology, 31*(6), 677–702. https://doi.org/10.1177/0022022100031006002.

Kagan, J. (1998). Biology and the child. In W. Damon & N. Eisenberg (Eds.), *Handbook of child psychology: Social, emotional, and personality development* (pp. 177–235). Hoboken, NJ: John Wiley.

Kagan, J., Snidman, N., Kahn, V., & Towsley, S. (2007). The preservation of two infant temperaments into adolescence: III. The current study. *Monographs of the Society for Research in Child Development, 72*, 19–30. https://doi.org/10.1111/j.1540-5834.2007.00429.x.

Kagitçibasi, C. (2012). Sociocultural change and integrative syntheses in human development: Autonomous-related self and social-cognitive competence. *Child Development Perspectives, 6*(1), 5–11. https://doi.org/10.1111/j.1750-8606.2011.00173.x.

Kawabata, Y., & Crick, N. R. (2013). Relational and physical aggression, peer victimization, and adjustment problems in Asian American and European American children. *Asian American Journal of Psychology, 4*(3), 211–216. https://doi.org/10.1037/a0031205.

Kawabata, Y., Tseng, W. L., Murray-Close, D., & Crick, N. R. (2012). Developmental trajectories of Chinese children's relational and physical aggression: Associations with social-psychological adjustment problems. *Journal of Abnormal Child Psychology, 40*(7), 1087–1097. https://doi.org/10.1007/s10802-012-9633-8.

Keller, H. (2020). Children's socioemotional development across cultures. *Annual Review of Developmental Psychology, 2*, 27–46. https://doi.org/10.1146/annurev-devpsych-033020-031552.

Kho, C., Main, A., Chung, S., & Zhou, Q. (2019). Intrusive parenting in Chinese American immigrant families: Relations with cultural orientations and children's adjustment. *Asian American Journal of Psychology, 10*(4), 341–350. https://doi.org/10.1037/aap0000165.

Kim, Y.-H., Cohen, D., & Au, W.-T. (2010). The jury and abjury of my peers: The self in face and dignity cultures. *Journal of Personality and Social Psychology, 98*(6), 904–916. https://doi.org/10.1037/a0017936.

Kindermann, T. A., & Gest, S. D. (2018). The peer group: Linking conceptualizations, theories, and methods. In W. M. Bukowski, B. Laursen, & K. H. Rubin (Eds.), *Handbook of peer interactions, relationships, and groups* (pp. 84–105). New York: Guilford Press.

Kong, X., Brook, C. A., Zhong, J., Liu, J., & Schmidt, L. A. (2022). Are cross-cultural shyness comparisons valid? Testing invariance with multigroup CFA and the alignment method across eastern and western cultures. *Psychological Assessment, 34*(3), 271–280. https://doi.org/10.1037/pas0001086.

Kopp, C. B. (1982). Antecedents of self-regulation: A developmental perspective. *Developmental Psychology, 18*(2), 199–214. https://doi.org/10.1037/0012-1649.18.2.199.

Köster, M., Schuhmacher, N., & Kärtner, J. (2015). A cultural perspective on prosocial development. *Human Ethology Bulletin, 30*, 71–82.

Kou, Y., Fu, Y., & Zhang Q. (2007). The prosocial behaviors endorsed by adolescents: A focus group study. *Sociological Studies, 3*, 154–173.

Kou, Y., Yan, F., & Ma, Y. (2004). The prosocial behaviors endorsed by junior middle school students. *Psychological Development and Education, 20*(4), 43–48. www.devpsy.com.cn/CN/Y2004/V20/I4/43.

Kou, Y., & Zhang, Q. (2006). Conceptual representation of early adolescents' prosocial behavior. *Sociological Studies, 5*, 169–187.

Kuang, Y., Wang, F., & Wang, Z.-J. (2021). Social class and children's prosociality: A study in the context of china's dual urban–rural structure. *Social Psychological and Personality Science, 12*(1), 63–70. https://doi.org/10.1177/1948550619887698.

LaFontana, K. M., & Cillessen, A. H. N. (2002). Children's perceptions of popular and unpopular peers: A multimethod assessment. *Developmental Psychology, 38*(5), 635–647. https://doi.org/10.1037/0012-1649.38.5.635.

Lan, X., Legare, C. H., Ponitz, C. C., Li, S., & Morrison, F. J. (2011). Investigating the links between the subcomponents of executive function and academic achievement: A cross-cultural analysis of Chinese and American preschoolers. *Journal of Experimental Child Psychology, 108*(3), 677–692. https://doi.org/10.1016/j.jecp.2010.11.001.

Lansford, J. E., Godwin, J., Bornstein, M. et al. (2018). Parenting, culture, and the development of externalizing behaviors from age 7 to 14 in nine countries. *Development and Psychopathology, 30*(5), 1937–1958. https://doi.org/10.1017/S0954579418000925.

Lansford, J. E., Skinner, A. T., Sorbring, E. et al. (2012). Boys' and girls' relational and physical aggression in nine countries. *Aggressive Behavior, 38* (4), 298–308. https://doi.org/10.1002/ab.21433.

Larson, R. (1999). On the uses of loneliness in adolescence. In K. Rotenberg & S. Hymel (Eds.), *Loneliness in childhood and adolescence* (pp. 244–262). New York: Cambridge Press.

Larson, R. W. (1997). The emergence of solitude as a constructive domain of experience in early adolescence. *Child Development, 68*(1), 80–93. https://doi.org/10.2307/1131927.

Lee, E.H., Zhou, Q., Eisenberg, N., & Wang, Y. (2013). Bidirectional relations between temperament and parenting styles in Chinese children. *International Journal of Behavioral Development, 37*(1), 57–67. https://doi.org/10.1177/0165025412460795.

Lei, H., Zhang, Q., Li, X. et al. (2019). Cumulative risk and problem behaviors among Chinese left-behind children: A moderated mediation model. *School Psychology International, 40*(3), 309–328. https://doi.org/10.1177/0143034319835255.

Leung, J. T. Y., & Shek, D. T. L. (2015). Parental beliefs and parental sacrifice of Chinese parents experiencing economic disadvantage in Hong Kong: Implications for social work. *British Journal of Social Work, 45*(4), 1119–1136. https://doi.org/10.1093/bjsw/bct190.

Leung, J. T. Y., & Shek, D. T. L. (2016). The influence of parental beliefs on the development of Chinese adolescents experiencing economic disadvantage: Maternal control as a mediator. *Journal of Family Issues, 37*(4), 543–573. https://doi.org/10.1177/0192513X13518776.

LeVine, R. A. (1988). Human parental care: Universal goals, cultural strategies, individual behavior. In R. A. LeVine, P. M. Miller, & M. M. West (Eds.), *New Directions for child development series: Parental behavior in diverse societies* (Vol. 40, pp. 3–12). San Francisco, CA: Jossey-Bass.

Li, Q., Zhang, W., & Zhao, J. (2021). The longitudinal associations among grandparent-grandchild cohesion, cultural beliefs about adversity, and depression in Chinese rural left-behind children. *Journal of Health Psychology, 26*(1), 140–155. https://doi.org/10.1177/1359105318803708.

Liu, J., Chen, X., Coplan, R. J. et al. (2015). Shyness and unsociability and their relations with adjustment in Chinese and Canadian children. *Journal of Cross-Cultural Psychology, 46*(3), 371–386. https://doi.org/10.1177/0022022114 567537.

Liu, J., Chen, X., Zhou, Y. et al. (2017). Relations of shyness–sensitivity and unsociability with adjustment in middle childhood and early adolescence in suburban Chinese children. *International Journal of Behavioral Development, 41*(6), 681–687. https://doi.org/10.1177/0165025416664195.

Liu, J., Li, D., Purwono, U., Chen, X., & French, D. C. (2015). Loneliness of Indonesian and Chinese adolescents as predicted by relationships with friends and parents. *Merrill-Palmer Quarterly, 61*(3), 362–382. https://doi .org/10.13110/merrpalmquar1982.61.3.0362.

Liu, J., & Wang, Q. (2018). Stressful life events and the development of integrity of rural-to-urban migrant children: The moderating role of social support and beliefs about adversity. *Psychological Development and Education, 34*(5), 548–557. https://doi.org/10.16187/j.cnki.issn1001-4918.2018.05.05.

Liu, J., Xiao, B., Coplan, R. J., Chen, X., & Li, D. (2018). Cross-lagged panel analyses of child shyness, maternal and paternal authoritarian parenting, and teacher-child relationships in Mainland China. *Journal of Child and Family Studies, 27*(12), 4116–4125. https://doi.org/10.1007/s10826-018-1229-7.

Liu, M., Chen, X., Fu, R., Li, D., & Liu, J. (2023). Social, academic, and psychological characteristics of peer groups in Chinese children: Same-domain and cross-domain effects on individual development. *Developmental Psychology, 59*(1), 57–68. https://doi.org/10.1037/ dev0001449.

Liu, X., Fu, R., Li, D., Liu, J., & Chen, X. (2018). Self- and group-orientations and adjustment in urban and rural chinese children. *Journal of Cross-Cultural Psychology, 49*(9), 1440–1456. https://doi.org/10.1177/ 0022022118795294.

Liu, Y.-L., & Chang, H.-T. (2016). The role of effortful control in the relationships among parental control, intentional self-regulation, and adolescent obedience. *Journal of Child and Family Studies, 25*(8), 2435–2446. https:// doi.org/10.1007/s10826-016-0405-x.

Louie, J. Y., Oh, B. J., & Lau, A. S. (2013). Cultural differences in the links between parental control and children's emotional expressivity. *Cultural Diversity and Ethnic Minority Psychology, 19*(4), 424–434. https://doi.org/ 10.1037/a0032820.

Luo, G. (1996). *Chinese traditional social and moral ideas and rules.* Beijing: The University of Chinese People Press.

Luthar, S. S., Ciciolla, L., & Suh, B. C. (2021). Adverse childhood experiences among youth from high-achieving schools: Appraising vulnerability processes toward fostering resilience. *American Psychologist, 76*(2), 300–313. https://doi.org/10.1037/amp0000754.

Luthar, S. S., Crossman, E. J., & Small, P. J. (2015). Resilience in the face of adversities. In M. E. Lamb & R. M. Lerner (Eds.), *Handbook of child psychology and developmental science: Socioemotional processes* (pp. 247–286). Hoboken, NJ: John Wiley.

Luthar, S. S., & Latendresse, S. J. (2005). Children of the affluent: Challenges to well-being. *Current Directions in Psychological Science, 14*(1), 49–53. https://doi.org/10.1111/j.0963-7214.2005.00333.x.

Ma, F., Heyman, G. D., Xiao, L. et al. (2019). Modesty can promote trust: Evidence from China. *Social Development, 28*(1), 218–233. https://doi.org/10.1111/sode.12327.

Maccoby, E. E., & Martin, J. A. (1983). Socialization in the context of the family: Parent–child interaction. In P. H. Mussen (Series Ed.) & E. M. Hetherington (Vol. Ed.), *Handbook of child psychology: Socialization, personality, and social development* (4th ed., Vol. 4., pp. 1–101). New York: Wiley.

Malti, T., Gummerum, M., Ongley, S. et al. (2016). "Who is worthy of my generosity?" Recipient characteristics and the development of children's sharing. *International Journal of Behavioral Development, 40*(1), 31–40. https://doi.org/10.1177/0165025414567007.

Masten, A. S. (2011). Resilience in children threatened by extreme adversity: Frameworks for research, practice, and translational synergy. *Development and Psychopathology, 23*(2), 493–506. https://doi.org/10.1017/S0954579411000198.

Miller, J. G., Wice, M., & Goyal, N. (2018). Contributions and challenges of cultural research on the development of social cognition. *Developmental Review, 50*(7), 65–76. https://doi.org/10.1016/j.dr.2018.03.003.

Mischel, W., Cantor, N., & Feldman, S. (1996). Principles of self-regulation: The nature of willpower and self-control. In E. T. Higgins & A. W. Kruglanski (Eds.), *Social psychology: Handbook of basic principles* (pp. 329–360). New York: Guilford.

Muhtadie, L., Zhou, Q., Eisenberg, N., & Wang, Y. (2013). Predicting internalizing problems in Chinese children: the unique and interactive effects of parenting and child temperament. *Development and Psychopathology, 25*(3), 653–667. https://doi.org/10.1017/S0954579413000084.

Murray, K. T., & Kochanska, G. (2002). Effortful control: Factor structure and relation to externalizing and internalizing behaviors. *Journal of Abnormal*

Child Psychology, *30*(5), 503–514. https://doi.org/10.1023/a:1019821
031523.

Navon, R., & Ramsey, P. G. (1989). Possession and exchange of materials in
Chinese and American preschools. *Journal of Research in Childhood
Education*, *4*(1), 18–29. https://doi.org/10.1080/02568548909594942.

Ng, F. F. Y., Pomerantz, E. M., & Deng, C. (2014). Why are Chinese mothers
more controlling than American mothers? "My child is my report card."
Child development, *85*(1), 355–369. https://doi.org/10.1111/cdev.12102.

Ng, F. F.-Y., Pomerantz, E. M., & Lam, S.-f. (2007). European American and
Chinese parents' responses to children's success and failure: Implications for
children's responses. *Developmental Psychology*, *43*(5), 1239–1255. https://
doi.org/10.1037/0012-1649.43.5.1239.

Ng, F. F. Y. & Wang, Q. (2019). Asian and Asian American parenting. In
M. H. Bornstein (Ed.), *Handbook of parenting: Social conditions and applied
parenting* (pp. 108–169). New York: Routledge.

Orlick, T., Zhou, Q.-y., & Partington, J. (1990). Co-operation and conflict
within Chinese and Canadian kindergarten settings. *Canadian Journal of
Behavioural Science / Revue canadienne des sciences du comportement*, *22*
(1), 20–25. https://doi.org/10.1037/h0078933.

Oyserman, D., Coon, H. M., & Kemmelmeier, M. (2002). Rethinking individualism and collectivism: Evaluation of theoretical assumptions and
meta-analyses. *Psychological Bulletin*, *128*(1), 3–72. https://doi.org/10.1037/
0033-2909.128.1.3.

Piaget, J. (1932). *The moral judgment of the child*. San Diego, CA: Harcourt, Brace.

Prior, M., Smart, D., Sanson, A., & Oberklaid, F. (2000). Does shy-inhibited
temperament in childhood lead to anxiety problems in adolescence? *Journal
of the American Academy of Child & Adolescent Psychiatry*, *39*(4), 461–468.
https://doi.org/10.1097/00004583-200004000-00015.

Putnick, D. L., & Bornstein, M. H. (2016). Measurement invariance conven-
tions and reporting: The state of the art and future directions for psychological research. *Developmental Review*, *41*, 71–90. https://doi.org/10.1016/
j.dr.2016.06.004.

Rao, N., & Stewart, S. M. (1999). Cultural influences on sharer and recipient
behavior: Sharing in Chinese and Indian preschool children. *Journal of
Cross-Cultural Psychology*, *30*(2), 219–241. https://doi.org/10.1177/
0022022199030002005.

Rapee, R. M., Kim, J., Wang, J. et al. (2011). Perceived impact of socially anxious
behaviors on individuals' lives in Western and East Asian countries. *Behavior
Therapy*, *42*(3), 485–492. https://doi.org/10.1016/j.beth.2010.11.004.

Rodkin, P. C., Farmer, T. W., Pearl, R., & Van Acker, R. (2000). Heterogeneity of popular boys: Antisocial and prosocial configurations. *Developmental Psychology*, *36*(1), 14–24. https://doi.org/10.1037/0012-1649.36.1.14.

Rohner, R. P., & Lansford, J. E. (2017). Deep structure of the human affectional system: Introduction to interpersonal acceptance–rejection theory. *Journal of Family Theory & Review*, *9*(4), 426–440. https://doi.org/10.1111/jftr.12219.

Rose, A. J., Swenson, L. P., & Waller, E. M. (2004). Overt and relational aggression and perceived popularity: Developmental differences in concurrent and prospective relations. *Developmental Psychology*, *40*(3), 378–387. https://doi.org/10.1037/0012-1649.40.3.378.

Rothbart, M. K. (2011). *Becoming who we are: Temperament and personality in development*. New York: Guilford Press.

Rudolph, K. D., & Conley, C. S. (2005). The socioemotional costs and benefits of social-evaluative concerns: Do girls care too much? *Journal of Personality*, *73* (1), 115–138.https://doi.org/10.1111/j.1467-6494.2004.00306.x.

Rubin, K. H., Bukowski, W. M., & Bowker, J. C. (2015). Children in peer groups. In M. H. Bornstein, T. Leventhal, & R. M. Lerner (Eds.), *Handbook of child psychology and developmental science: Ecological settings and processes* (pp. 175–222). Hoboken, NJ: John Wiley.

Rubin, K. H., Chen, X., McDougall, P., Bowker, A., & McKinnon, J. (1995). The waterloo longitudinal Project: Predicting internalizing and externalizing problems in adolescence. *Development and Psychopathology*, *7*(4), 751–764. https://doi.org/10.1017/S0954579400006829.

Rubin, K. H., Coplan, R. J., & Bowker, J. (2009). Social withdrawal in childhood. *Annual Review of Psychology*, 60, 141–171.

Rutter, M. (1987). Psychosocial resilience and protective mechanisms. *American Journal of Orthopsychiatry*, *57*(3), 316–331. https://doi.org/10.1111/j.1939-0025.1987.tb03541.x.

Rutter, M. (2012). Resilience as a dynamic concept. *Development and Psychopathology*, *24*(2), 335–344. https://doi.org/10.1017/S0954579412000028.

Sang, B., Ding, X., Coplan, R. J. et al. (2018). Assessment and implications of social avoidance in Chinese early adolescents. *Journal of Early Adolescence*, *38*(4), 554–573. https://doi.org/10.1177/0272431616678988.

Schirmbeck, K., Rao, N., & Maehler, C. (2020). Similarities and differences across countries in the development of executive functions in children: A systematic review. *Infant and Child Development*, *29*(1), e2164. https://doi.org/10.1002/icd.2164.

Sharabany, R. (2006). The cultural context of children and adolescents: Peer relationships and intimate friendships among Arab and Jewish children in

Israel. In X. Chen, D. French, & B. Schneider (Eds.), *Peer relationships in cultural context* (pp.452–478). New York: Cambridge University Press.

Shen, J., Liu, X., Zhao, J., & Shi, B. (2015). The psychological development of Chinese left-behind children and migrant children in urbanization process. *Psychological Development and Education*, *31*(1), 108–116. https://doi.org/10.16187/j.cnki.issn1001-4918.2015.01.15.

Shen, J. J., Cheah, C. S. L., & Yu, J. (2018). Asian American and European American emerging adults' perceived parenting styles and self-regulation ability. *Asian American Journal of Psychology*, *9*(2), 140–148. https://doi.org/10.1037/aap0000099

Somerville, L. H. (2013). Special issue on the teenage brain: Sensitivity to social evaluation. *Current Directions in Psychological Science*, *22*(2), 121–127. https://doi.org/10.1177/0963721413476512.

Song, Y., Malhotra, S., Broekhuizen, M. et al. (2021). Prosocial behavior in young preschoolers: A cross-cultural study across The Netherlands, India, and China. *The Journal of Genetic Psychology*, *182*(3), 129–148.... https://doi.org/10.1080/00221325.2021.1891857.

Spithoven, A. W. M., Bastin, M., Bijttebier, P., & Goossens, L. (2018). Lonely adolescents and their best friend: An examination of loneliness and friendship quality in best friendship dyads. *Journal of Child and Family Studies*, *27*, 3598–3605. https://doi.org/10.1007/s10826-018-1183-4.

Stevenson, H. W., Lee, S.- y., Chen, C. et al. (1990). Contexts of achievement: A study of American, Chinese, and Japanese children. *Monographs of the Society for Research in Child Development*, *55*(1–2)[221], 123. https://doi.org/10.2307/1166090.

Stewart, S. M., Bond, M. H., Kennard, B. D., Ho, L. M., & Zaman, R. M. (2002). Does the Chinese construct of guan export to the West? *International Journal of Psychology*, *37*(2), 74–82. https://doi.org/10.1080/0020759014 3000162.

Stewart, S. M., & McBride-Chang, C. (2000). Influences on children's sharing in a multicultural setting. *Journal of Cross-Cultural Psychology*, *31*(3), 333–348. https://doi.org/10.1177/0022022100031003003.

Stewart, S. M., Rao, N., Bond, M. H. et al. (1998). Chinese dimensions of parenting: Broadening western predictors and outcomes. *International Journal of Psychology*, *33*(5), 345–358. https://doi.org/10.1080/002075998 400231.

Sullivan, H. S. (1953). *The interpersonal theory of psychiatry*. New York: W W Norton.

Talhelm, T., Zhang, X., Oishi, S. et al. (2014). Large-scale psychological differences within China explained by rice versus wheat agriculture. *Science*, 344, 603–608. https://doi.org/10.1126/science.1246850.

Tani, F., Ponti, L., & Smorti, M. (2014). Shyness and psychological adjustment during adolescence: The moderating role of parenting style. *The Open Psychology Journal*, 7, Article 33–44. https://doi.org/10.2174/187435010140 7010033.

Teng, Z., Liu, Y., & Guo, C. (2015). A meta-analysis of the relationship between self-esteem and aggression among Chinese students. *Aggression and Violent Behavior*, 21, 45–54. https://doi.org/10.1016/j.avb.2015.01.005.

Tobin, J. J., Wu, D. Y. H., & Davidson, D. H. (1989). *Preschool in three cultures*. New Haven, CT: Yale University Press.

Triandis, H. C., Bontempo, R., Villareal, M. J., Asai, M., & Lucca, N. (1988). Individualism and collectivism: Cross-cultural perspectives on self-ingroup relationships. *Journal of Personality and Social Psychology*, 54(2), 323–338. https://doi.org/10.1037/0022-3514.54.2.323.

Tseng, W. L., Banny, A. M., Kawabata, Y., Crick, N. R., & Gau, S. S. (2013). A cross-lagged structural equation model of relational aggression, physical aggression, and peer status in a Chinese culture. *Aggressive Behavior*, 39 (4), 301–315. https://doi.org/10.1002/ab.21480.

Van den Berg, Y., Lansu, T. A. M., & Cillessen, A. (2015). Measuring social status and social behavior with peer and teacher nomination methods. *Social Development*, 24(4), 815–832. https://doi.org/10.1111/sode.12120.

Van Doesum, N. J., Tybur, J. M., & Van Lange, P. A. (2017). Class impressions: Higher social class elicits lower prosociality. *Journal of Experimental Social Psychology*, 68, 11−20. https://doi.org/10.1016/j.jesp.2016.06.001.

Vaughn, B. E., & Santos, A. J. (2007). An evolutionary/ecological account of aggressive behavior and trait aggression in human children and adolescents. In P. H. Hawley, T. D. Little, & P. C. Rodkin (Eds.), *Aggression and adaptation: The bright side to bad behavior* (pp. 31–63). Dallas, TX: Lawrence Erlbaum Associates.

Volbrecht, M. M., & Goldsmith, H. H. (2010). Early temperamental and family predictors of shyness and anxiety. *Developmental Psychology*, 46(5), 1192–1205. https://doi.org/10.1037/a0020616.

Vygotsky, L. S. (1978). *Mind in society: The development of higher psychological processes*. Cambridge, MA: Harvard University Press.

Wang, L., & Mesman, J. (2015). Child development in the face of rural-to-urban migration in China: A meta-analytic review. *Perspectives on Psychological Science*, 10(6), 813–831. https://doi.org/10.1177/1745691615600145.

Wang, Q. (2008). Emotion knowledge and autobiographical memory across the preschool years: A cross-cultural longitudinal investigation. *Cognition, 108* (1), 117–135. https://doi.org/10.1016/j.cognition.2008.02.002.

Wang, S., Zhang, W., Li, D. et al. (2015). Forms of aggression, peer relationships, and relational victimization among Chinese adolescent girls and boys: Roles of prosocial behavior. *Frontiers in Psychology, 6,* Article 1264.

Wang, Y., Tang, Y.-Y., & Wang, J. (2015). Cultural differences in donation decision-making. *PLoS ONE, 10*(9), e0138219. https://doi.org/10.1371/journal.pone.0138219.

Way, N. (2006). The cultural practice of close friendships among urban adolescents in the United States. In X. Chen, D. French, & B. Schneider (Eds.), *Peer relationships in cultural context* (pp. 403–425). New York: Cambridge University Press.

Wen, M., & Lin, D. (2012). Child development in rural China: Children left behind by their migrant parents and children of nonmigrant families. *Child Development, 83*(1), 120–136. https://doi.org/10.1111/j.1467-8624.2011.01698.x.

Westenberg, P. M., Drewes, M. J., Goedhart, A. W., Siebelink, B. M., & Treffers, P. D. A. (2004). A developmental analysis of self-reported fears in late childhood through mid-adolescence: Social-evaluative fears on the rise? *Journal of Child Psychology and Psychiatry, 45*(3), 481–495. https://doi.org/10.1111/j.1469-7610.2004.00239.x.

Whiting, B. B., & Edwards, C. P. (1988). *Children of different worlds: The formation of social behavior.* Cambridge, MA: Harvard University Press.

The World Factbook (2022). *Explore all countries: China.* www.cia.gov/the-world-factbook/countries/china/.

Wu, C., & Chao, R. K. (2005). Intergenerational cultural conflicts in norms of parental warmth among Chinese American immigrants. *International Journal of Behavioral Development, 29*(6), 516–523. https://doi.org/10.1080/01650250500147444.

Wu, P., Robinson, C. C., Yang, C. et al. (2002). Similarities and differences in mothers' parenting of preschoolers in China and the United States. *International Journal of Behavioral Development, 26*(6), 481–491. https://doi.org/10.1080/01650250143000436.

Wurster, T., & Xie, H. (2014). Aggressive and prosocial behaviors: The social success of bistrategic preadolescents. *International Journal of Behavioral Development, 38*(4), 367–377. https://doi.org/10.1177/0165025414531463

Xiao, B., Bullock, A., Coplan, R. J., Liu, J., & Cheah, C. S. L. (2021). Exploring the relations between parenting practices, child shyness, and internalizing problems in Chinese culture. *Journal of Family Psychology, 35*(6), 833–843. https://doi.org/10.1037/fam0000904.

Xu, Y., Farver, J. A. M., Chang, L., Zhang, Z., & Yu, L. (2007). Moving away or fitting in? Understanding shyness in Chinese children. *Merrill-Palmer Quarterly, 53*(4), 527–556. https://doi.org/10.1353/mpq.2008.0005.

Xu, Y., Farver, J. A. M., Yu, L., & Zhang, Z. (2009a). Three types of shyness in Chinese children and the relation to effortful control. *Journal of Personality and Social Psychology, 97*(6), 1061–1073. https://doi.org/10.1037/a0016576.

Xu, Y., Farver, J. A. M., & Zhang, Z. (2009b). Temperament, harsh and indulgent parenting, and Chinese children's proactive and reactive aggression. *Child Development, 80*(1), 244–258. https://doi.org/10.1111/j.1467-8624.2008.01257.x.

Xu, Y., & Krieg, A. (2014). Shyness in Asian American children and the relation to temperament, parents' acculturation, and psychosocial functioning. *Infant and Child Development, 23*(3), 333–342. https://doi.org/10.1002/icd.1860.

Xu, Y., & Zhang, Z. (2008). Distinguishing proactive and reactive aggression in Chinese children. *Journal of Abnormal Child Psychology, 36*(4), 539–552. https://doi.org/10.1007/s10802-007-9198-0.

Yan, J., Zhang, W., & Cui, J. (2016). Relation of mother's parenting style to self-esteem and shyness in adolescents. *Chinese Mental Health Journal, 30,* 142–147.

Yang, F., Chen, X., & Wang, L. (2015). Shyness-sensitivity and social, school, and psychological adjustment in urban Chinese children: A four-wave longitudinal study. *Child Development, 86*(6), 1848–1864. www.jstor.org/stable/24698580.

Yang, Y., Kong, X., Guo, Z., & Kou, Y. (2021). Can self-compassion promote gratitude and prosocial behavior in adolescents? A 3-year longitudinal study from China. *Mindfulness, 12,* 1377–1386. https://doi.org/10.1007/s12671-021-01605-9.

Yang, Y., Zhang, M., & Kou, Y. (2016). The revalidation and development of the prosocial behavior scale for adolescent. *Chinese Social Psychological Review, 10,* 135–150.

Yang, Z., Fu, X., Yu, X., & Lv, Y. (2018). Longitudinal relations between adolescents' materialism and prosocial behavior toward family, friends, and strangers. *Journal of Adolescence, 62,* 162–170. https://doi.org/10.1016/j.adolescence.2017.11.013.

Yu, J., Cheah, C. S., Hart, C. H., Yang, C., & Olsen, J. A. (2019). Longitudinal effects of maternal love withdrawal and guilt induction on Chinese American preschoolers' bullying aggressive behavior. *Development and Psychopathology, 31*(4), 1467–1475. https://doi.org/10.1017/S0954579418001049.

Zhang, L., & Eggum-Wilkens, N. D. (2018). Correlates of shyness and unsociability during early adolescence in urban and rural China. *The Journal of Early Adolescence*, *38*(3), 408–421. https://doi.org/10.1177/0272431616670993.

Zhang M.-R., & Ng F. F.-Y. (2022). Chinese adolescents' perceptions of parental socialization goals: Variations by ethnicity and gender. *The Journal of Early Adolescence*, 42(8), 995–1025. https://doi.org/10.1177/027243162210 88749.

Zhang, W., & Fuligni, A. J. (2006). Authority, autonomy, and family relationships among adolescents in urban and rural China. *Journal of Research on Adolescence*, *16*(4), 527–537. https://doi.org/10.1111/j.1532-7795.2006 .00506.x

Zhang, Z., & Xu, Y. (2019). Implicit theories of shyness in American and Chinese children. *European Journal of Social Psychology*, *49*(1), 200–210. https://doi.org/10.1002/ejsp.2510.

Zhao, J., Liu, X., & Zhang, W. (2013). Peer rejection, peer acceptance and psychological adjustment of left-behind children: The roles of parental cohesion and children's cultural beliefs about adversity. *Acta Psychologica Sinica*, *45*(7), 797−810. https://doi.org/10.3724/SP.J.1041.2013.00797.

Zhao, L., Li, D., Xu, X., Wang, Y., & Sun, W. (2016). The roles of educational values and Chinese cultural beliefs about adversity in the relationship between family financial strain and academic achievement among middle school students. *Psychological Development and Education*, *32*(4), 409–417. https://doi.org/10.16187/j.cnki.issn1001-4918.2016.04.04.

Zhong, B. L., Ding, J., Chen, H. H. et al. (2013). Depressive disorders among children in the transforming China: An epidemiological survey of prevalence, correlates, and service use. *Depression and Anxiety*, *30*(9), 881–892. https://doi.org/10.1002/da.22109.

Zhong, J., Liu, J., Xu, G. et al. (2021). Measurement invariance of two different short forms of social interaction anxiety scale (SIAS) and social phobia scale (SPS) in Chinese and US samples. *European Journal of Psychological Assessment*. Advance online publication. https://doi.org/10.1027/1015-5759/ a000689.

Zhou, C., Yiu, V., Wu, M., & Greenfield, P. M. (2018). Perception of cross-generational differences in child behavior and parent socialization: A mixed-method interview study with grandmothers in China. *Journal of Cross-Cultural Psychology*, *49*(1), 62–81. https://doi.org/10.1177/2F002202211 .7736029.

Zhou, Q., Lengua, L. J., & Wang, Y. (2009). The relations of temperament reactivity and effortful control to children's adjustment problems in China

and the United States. *Developmental Psychology, 45*(3), 724–739. https://
doi.org/10.1037/a0013776.

Zhou, Z., Qu, Y., & Li, X. (2022). Parental collectivism goals and Chinese
adolescents' prosocial behaviors: The mediating role of authoritative parenting. *Journal of Youth and Adolescence, 51*(4), 766–779. https://doi.org/
10.1007/s10964-022-01579-4.

Zimmer-Gembeck, M. J., Geiger, T. C., & Crick, N. R. (2005). Relational and
physical aggression, prosocial behavior, and peer relations: Gender moder-
ation and bidirectional associations. *The Journal of Early Adolescence,
25*(4), 421–452. https://doi.org/10.1177/0272431605279841.

Cambridge Elements ᐧ

Child Development

Marc H. Bornstein

Eunice Kennedy Shriver National Institute of Child Health and Human Development,
Bethesda Institute for Fiscal Studies, London
UNICEF, New York City

Marc H. Bornstein is an Affiliate of the *Eunice Kennedy Shriver* National Institute of Child
Health and Human Development, an International Research Fellow at the Institute for Fiscal
Studies (London), and UNICEF Senior Advisor for Research for ECD Parenting Programmes.
Bornstein is President Emeritus of the Society for Research in Child Development,
Editor Emeritus of *Child Development*, and founding Editor of *Parenting:*
Science and Practice.

About the Series

Child development is a lively and engaging, yet serious and real-world subject of scientific
study that encompasses myriad theories, methods, substantive areas, and applied
concerns. Cambridge Elements in Child Development addresses many contemporary
topics in child development with unique, comprehensive, and state-of-the-art
treatments of principal issues, primary currents of thinking, original perspectives, and
empirical contributions to understanding early human development.

Cambridge Elements ≡

Child Development